ENGLAND IN EUROPE
1066–1453

ENGLAND IN EUROPE
1066–1453

Edited by
NIGEL SAUL

St. Martin's Press
NEW YORK

First published in the United States of America 1994

ISBN 0–312–12155–5

Library of Congress Cataloging-in-Publication Data

England in Europe, 1066–1453 / edited by Nigel Saul.
    p. cm.
    Includes bibliographical references (p. 166) and index.
    ISBN 0–312–12155–5
    1. Europe—Relations—Great Britain.   2. Great Britain—Relations—
Europe.   3. Great Britain—History—Medieval period. 1066–1485.
I. Saul, Nigel.
D34.G7E54   1994
942—dc20

Conceived, edited and designed by Collins & Brown Limited

Commissioning Editor: Juliet Gardiner
Designed by: Claire Graham

Typeset by J&L Composition Ltd, Filey, North Yorkshire
Printed and bound in Finland

Cover illustration: William the Conqueror and his barons: from a
fourteenth-century manuscript (British Museum/Weidenfeld &
Nicolson Archives)

CONTENTS

PREFACE

OVER THE PAST THREE YEARS the pace of change in Europe has been quicker than at any time since the end of the Second World War. In the west of the Continent there have been major developments in the European Community leading to the elimination of internal barriers and the creation of the Single Internal Market, while at the same time east of the Elbe the once seemingly monolithic Soviet empire has collapsed and the former satellite states have been left to find their own individual destinies in the world. Rarely has the political scene in Europe been so vibrant and so unpredictable — or indeed so exciting.

These events have had a major effect on our perception of the past and on the way in which we come to terms with it. Suddenly, the realization has dawned that history did not come to an end in 1945, that the European order was not frozen in stone at Potsdam and Yalta. Familiar themes have re-emerged to haunt us again — themes such as nationalism, separatism and the balance of power. So far from history coming to an end, as Francis Fukuyama once supposed that it had, the opposite has been the case; history has started again; it has resumed its old and familiar patterns.

In Britain, these considerations about the relationship of the present to the past have been lent added force by recent developments in the Community — in particular by the debates about political and economic union. Questions have been asked about the country's role in the world and about the background to her relations with Europe. How close were those relations in the past? To what extent was England's historical development peculiar to herself? To what extent has the Channel been a barrier between the British Isles and Europe? ('A moat defensive to a house,' as John of Gaunt put it.) Has the Channel hindered or assisted communications between the two?

These are all questions which in their different ways open up historical perspectives on contemporary preoccupations; and they are all questions to which historians can offer a variety of insights and explanations. Implicitly or explicitly they are central to the purpose of the present book.

The book is not, of course, intended to be a direct intervention in the arguments currently being voiced about Britain and Europe: it has no particular axe to grind, least of all political, and the contributions to it espouse no particular outlook. Its purpose is simply to highlight the background to the issues and to set them in a perspective provided by a study of one period — the Middle Ages. The themes considered are varied. Analyses of England's relations with other states or peoples of Europe are interspersed with chronologically focused studies of particular episodes such as the Norman Conquest and the outbreak of the Hundred Years War. An introductory essay by the editor surveys the scene and highlights some of the issues discussed; while a discussion of the pre-Conquest period by Professor Nelson provides the essential background to what follows. There is no formal conclusion or attempt at summing up, because it is for the reader to reach his or her own conclusions on the basis of the evidence offered. Our twin aims are to inform and to stimulate — and to do so, we hope, in as lively and accessible a way as possible.

NIGEL SAUL

CHAPTER I

ENGLAND AND EUROPE: PROBLEMS AND POSSIBILITIES

Nigel Saul

O N THE HEREFORD WORLD MAP (*c.* 1280–90) the British Isles are
hardly conspicuous by their prominence. Squeezed into the bottom
left-hand quadrant, between Europe on the one hand and the map's
border on the other, they are easily overlooked altogether. Ireland is
reduced to little more than a sliver; the bulges of East Anglia are greatly
shrunken, and the south-western peninsula is completely dispensed with.
Even allowing for the problems caused by fitting the Isles into the arc of
the circle, it is clear that the Hereford artist — probably Richard de
Haldingham, a canon of the cathedral — had little interest in either their
location or their shape.

Earlier artists, however, had evinced even less interest. To them the
Isles were of no more than marginal significance; in the words of the
sixth-century writer, Isidore of Seville, they lay on the fringes of the
known world and were separated from it by the sea. In the fourth-
century map of Martianus Capella they were split into three — the islands
of Hibernia, Anglia and Thanet — and were scattered across the great
ocean that was thought to surround the (Roman) world. Gradually, over
time, they became incorporated into the main body of the map. On the
map of Henry of Mainz of *c.* 1110 two long islands are shown and on
a small psalter map of the mid-thirteenth century an attempt was made
to differentiate Scotland. But these improvements were largely cosmetic
in character. To most writers the British Isles were still of no more than
minor importance, and scarcely any interest was shown in attaining an
accurate representation of their outline.

The justification for this neglect is clear. The map-makers of antiquity
saw the world through Roman eyes. Rome provided the focal point of
their lives and everywhere else was judged in relation to it. On maps,
therefore, the city was placed prominently in the centre, with the

provinces ranged equidistant around it. As the antique world changed into the medieval, Rome's primacy came under challenge and new centres of religious and political power were established. In Christian epistemology Jerusalem supplanted Rome as the focal point of people's lives and therefore as the accepted centre of the known world. On the Hereford map it was shown at the point where the three continents intersected. Asia was placed above, in the upper semi-circle, Europe and Africa (their names reversed owing to scribal error) below, each occupying a quadrant. At the top, in the extreme east, was Paradise and, at the bottom, in the extreme west, the ocean beyond the Straits of Gibraltar.

The Hereford map was never intended to be a topographic representation of the world, of course: cartography in the modern sense was only in its infancy in the thirteenth century. The purpose of the map was rather cosmographic. Haldingham's idea was to tell the story of the world in its historical development and as an image of man's destiny. Drawing on a range of sources — the Bible, the bestiary, pagan philosophers, sagas and travellers' tales — he passed over a rich treasury of stories, among them the life of Alexander, the story of Adam and Eve, Noah's Ark and the Crucifixion. Through his presentation the map became a vivid chronicle of past events and a forceful exposition of Christian belief in God's total plan of Creation, man's fall and eventual salvation.

Given its strongly narrative character, the map is obviously of limited use as a source for medieval perceptions of topography. It gives little idea of how its author saw the shape of his own country or its relationship to others. Its view of the world is that of a theologian; its scale of values is clearly that of a theologian too. Attention is focused firmly on Jerusalem, the golden city, at the centre. In the European quadrant easily the most prominent city is Rome, because it was the seat of the papacy (it was honoured by the hexameter, 'Rome, Head of the Earth, holds the reins of the round world'). Scarcely inferior to Rome was Paris, a city important because it was the seat of Europe's oldest university, and universities were places for the study of God's dealings with men. Relegated to the fringes were the cities of Britain: Oxford rated a mention, as did such cathedral cities as Canterbury, York, Lincoln and Ely, but these were not major centres. Like the British Isles as a whole, they were of subordinate importance in what was essentially a theologically-inspired, God-centred view of the world.

Theologically inspired it may have been; but it was a view that was widely held at all levels of society in the Middle Ages. For most

Englishmen of the day the places that gave meaning to their lives lay far from their shores. Jerusalem, for example, though geographically on the fringes of the known world and since 1187 in Muslim hands, was the destination of the most important pilgrimage that they could make; people went there to die and to be buried. Rome, the burial place of St Peter and seat of the papacy, was the centre of the Church, which provided the framework for their lives and through which they hoped to secure salvation. Even Paris — though hardly a city of the same universal importance as the others — had a growing appeal as the seat of a monarchy (the Capetian) which was rapidly laying claim to the cultural leadership of Europe. What had England — and more to the point, what had Britain — to offer by comparison with centres like these? Perhaps, at the height of its fame, only the shrine of Becket at Canterbury.

Educated Englishmen with a sense of their kingdom's relative inferiority sought, whenever possible, to shake its soil from their feet. They made their way to France, to Capetian France, where they felt both happier and freer. John of Salisbury, a clerk in the household of Archbishop Theobald and one of the great scholars of his age, wrote eloquently of his feelings on reaching 'la belle France', 'la douce France' in 1164: 'After crossing the sea I seemed to feel the breath of a gentler breeze after our storms and tempests, and I admired with joy the wealth and abundance on all sides, and a people quiet and contented.' When he reached Paris, he was even more excited:

> Here, when I saw the abundance of food, the light-heartedness of the people, the respect paid to the clergy, the majesty and glory of the whole Church and the various employments of the seekers after truth, I looked on it as a veritable Jacob's ladder with its summit reaching to the skies and the angels ascending and descending. In the excitement of my happy pilgrimage I was forced to say, 'Truly the Lord is in this place and I knew it not.' Then that line of poetry came to my mind — 'Happy is the exile driven to this place.'

Other scholars had either preceded or were to follow John of Salisbury in his quest for fulfilment. Twelfth-century Englishmen were to be found in most of the major schools of Europe. They occupied positions of distinction in Paris and Bologna; they moved between the cathedral schools of Chartres and Laon, Rheims and Orléans. In academic terms, as Sir Richard Southern has written, England was a colony of the intellectual empire of France, and its colonial status was emphasized by the fact that, while nearly every English scholar of distinction went to France to study, no distinguished French scholars came to England, either to study or to teach.

On the other hand, to suggest that England in the twelfth century was entirely devoid of achievement would be wrong; for it was not. The schools of Oxford, Lincoln, London and Northampton were flourishing, and those at Oxford would develop into England's first university. At the same time a vigorous literature of government was coming into existence, its most famous products being the *Dialogue of the Exchequer* and Glanvill's *Treatise on the Laws of England*. In these and other areas there was ample evidence of vitality in England. Even so, it is still true that France was the more stimulating place to be in this period. Peter Abelard was teaching on the hill of Sainte-Geneviève near Paris; Abbot Suger was rebuilding the church of the royal abbey of St Denis; St Bernard was rousing the faithful with his call to a reformed Christian life. There was much going on to appeal to scholars from all over Europe — but not just to the scholars: to the nobility too. For them France was no less attractive than it was for the men of learning. It was the birthplace and chief centre of the cult of chivalry. It was the kingdom to which men instinctively turned for practice in the exercise of arms. According to the *Histoire de Guillaume le Maréchal*, the young marshal was told early on by his guardian, the chamberlain of Normandy, that it would serve him ill to stay in England; to experience the world of chivalry he should go to Normandy, to Brittany or to anywhere in northern France — there he would find tournaments once a fortnight in the season. The young man took his advice and, before he was twenty, had established a reputation for himself as one of the leading tiros in the field. Chauvency, Châlons and Lagny — these were the foremost tournament centres in Europe. Small wonder that to English chroniclers the tournament was known as the *conflictus Gallicus*.

In the twelfth century, of course, England's relationship with the French-speaking world was a particularly close and yet also particularly ambivalent one. Since the Norman Conquest in 1066 England had been part of a cross-Channel dominion ruled by the ducal dynasty of Normandy. The English aristocracy had been expropriated and replaced by one which was for long to see itself as Norman or Anglo-Norman in character. Socially, England and the northern parts of France were brought closer together than they had ever been, or were to be again. King and nobility regarded the two parts of the realm as one and sought to bring them together again when, as after 1087, they were temporarily separated. Yet, at the same time and by an opposite process of development, the imposition of alien rule and the disregard shown by the Normans for the traditions and customs of the English people encouraged a gradual reawakening of English identity. Culturally, in the twelfth century England and Normandy began to grow apart: the English found a new pride in their Anglo-Saxon past, and the Normans drifted into the orbit of Capetian Paris, as their reception of Parisian architectural styles shows. By the reign of John the two states were forging quite separate identities. John's loss of the duchy to the French can be seen in this sense as merely the final stage of a process of estrangement that had begun half or three-quarters of a century before.

The re-establishment of English identity in the thirteenth century, made possible or at least accelerated by the ending of the union with Normandy, did not mean that the country's ties with Europe in any way weakened. Socially and economically England — indeed, Britain — was fully part of what has been termed 'the medieval European community' and had been from the earliest times. A wealth of evidence from the pre-1066 period bears witness to this. Perhaps the most striking is from the Sutton Hoo ship burial in East Anglia, dating from roughly the mid-seventh century. Among the goods deposited with the king for his journey to the next world were Roman plate, Merovingian gold coins, silver spoons and a silver dish from Byzantium, and a great helmet stylistically of late-Roman and ultimately Sassanid origin: this half-pagan, half-Christian ruler, in other words (perhaps Redwald, king of the East Angles), had ties with Gaul, the Mediterranean and even the Byzantine Empire. He and his peers, though physically on the fringes of Europe, were locked into trading networks that extended through Europe into the Near East. Small wonder that a later ruler, Offa of Mercia (757–96) was able to bring pressure on the Emperor Charlemagne, whom he aspired to emulate, by threatening to cut off trade with the Frankish lands. Goods from England, in the form of furs, wool, woollen textiles and — not to be forgotten, slaves — were of vital importance to the well-being of merchants and their customers in many parts of the Continent.

Equally suggestive of England's integration into the wider European economy in the early Middle Ages are the religious and intellectual currents of the time. Through acceptance of Christianity in the seventh century England had become part of a great religious commonwealth whose centre was at Rome. A door was opened to ideas and influences which had their origins in the very different, and more urbanized, world of the Mediterranean. Absorbing these ideas was neither easy nor straightforward: the earliest missionaries, led by Augustine, found it difficult to adapt to local circumstances, and the Roman urban-based diocesan organization which they imposed on the country accorded ill with a largely rural society. By the 670s, however, these problems were being overcome. At the Synod of Whitby in 664, King Oswy of Northumbria had embraced the Roman obedience and, four years later, as if by way of setting the seal on the process of absorption, a Syrian, Theodore of Tarsus, was appointed Archbishop of Canterbury. He was to be one of the outstanding holders of that office in the Middle Ages.

It would be wrong to suppose that the traffic in men and ideas was entirely one way, however; it was not. In the 590s St Columbanus, an Irishman who had been a monk at Bangor, crossed to Gaul, settled there and founded a monastery at Luxeuil. A century later two Englishmen actively proselytized in the area of present-day Holland and north Germany. In the 690s one, a Northumbrian called Willibrord, established a bishopric among the Frisians and, in the early 700s, his younger contemporary, Boniface, a West Saxon, continuing his predecessor's work, preached in Germany and founded the great abbey of Fulda before meeting his death at the hands of the Frisians in 754. These were probably not the only missionaries working on the Continent at this time; there were surely others whose names have been lost, for this was a time when relations between Britain and the Continent were particularly close. It is in the context of this closeness of relations that England's role in the Renaissance of the seventh and eighth centuries is to be understood. The power-house of that Renaissance, the kingdom of Northumbria, where Bede lived and worked, stood at the centre of a culturally vibrant world. To the west lay Ireland with its flourishing monastic culture — a culture which produced such masterpieces as the Book of Durrow; to the north lay the Pictish kingdoms, which were deeply influenced by Irish monasticism; to the south-east lay the rich trading world of the Rhine estuary; and to the south directly were the English kingdoms which were already in close contact with Gaul and Rome. All these areas were easily accessible by sea routes. Small wonder that Northumbrian culture in this period exhibited influences from so many parts of Europe. And small wonder too that it was to a Northumbrian (albeit a Northumbrian abroad), Alcuin of York, that Charlemagne turned when he wanted to reinvigorate the religious and intellectual life of his own realms. The later eighth century was one of the few periods when the tide of ideas flowing from England to the Continent was stronger than that flowing in the other direction.

By the late 700s, when Alcuin was settling in Frankia, the finest days of the Northumbrian Renaissance lay in the past; the Viking raids, which began with an isolated attack on Lindisfarne in 793, were to deal a shattering blow to Northumbrian culture. Even before they came, however, the creative impulse in the kingdom was on the wane. The revival of learning known as the Carolingian Renaissance was claiming the cultural initiative for the Continent, and it was around Aachen and later the Île de France that, in cultural terms, Europe was to revolve in the central Middle Ages. England was never again in the medieval period to regain the centrality that she had enjoyed in the seventh and eighth centuries hence the consciousness of inferiority felt by the writers noted above. From this time on England's importance to her neighbours was to lie primarily in two quite different areas — her wealth, which made her a valued trading partner; and the martial valour of her kings, which made her a power feared by rulers both to the north and to the south.

The wealth for which England was renowned came from two main sources — her soil, which particularly in the midlands and the south was highly productive; and her sheep flocks, which were kept partly for meat but most of all for wool. The soil supported a pre-Black Death population of some 5–6 million in relative self-sufficiency: there were some years, notably 1315–16, when people starved for want of food, but generally there was little need for corn to be imported. The main earner of bullion for the country in the Middle Ages was wool. Great quantities were exported each year — roughly 25,000–30,000 sacks in the late thirteenth century, when the customs accounts begin, rising to 38,000 sacks between 1311 and 1313, and steadying at 10,000–20,000 in the late fourteenth and early fifteenth centuries. The main demand came from the cloth-making cities of Flanders and Italy. In Florence and Ypres, Ghent and Bruges English wool was valued for its high quality and fineness. Before the fourteenth century, the chief traders in the commodity were foreigners, particularly Italians whose role as agents for the collection of papal taxation enabled them to build up ties with every state in Europe. Bankruptcies and interruptions to trade in the early fourteenth century, resulting from war, allowed English merchants to step in, however, and by the 1360s the bulk of the trade was handled by a group known as the

Company of the Staple, who were granted a monopoly of the right to export in return for making loans to the Crown on the security of the customs imposed. The Company survived until the middle of the sixteenth century, but with the passage of time its position weakened. The tax on wool proved higher than the traffic would bear; foreigners turned elsewhere for their supplies of wool, notably to Spain, and the wool left unsold was made into cloth here. In other words, the unintended side-effect of the taxation of exports was to provide a tariff wall behind which a native cloth trade could take root and develop. By the end of the Middle Ages England had been transformed from a country relying on the export of a raw material to one trading in that of a manufactured good.

The history of the taxation of wool highlights the importance of the connection forged in late medieval England between trade and the finance of war. Without the revenue from the wool tax the Crown would have had far less to spend on war than it did. In the mid- to late fourteenth century some £30,000–£70,000 were reaped annually from this source. The king used this money to raise loans to pay his troops; he was able both to muster larger armies and to keep them in the field for longer than had commonly been the case before. English successes in the long struggle with France after 1337, known as the Hundred Years War, were the result in no small measure of the financial superiority of her rulers. Until the Valois kings responded by imposing taxation without consent on their subjects in the fifteenth century, the kings of England could spend double what their adversaries could on warfare.

English interest in warfare did not of course develop suddenly with her rulers' ability to tap trading wealth (though it greatly increased then); it had its origins much further back. In the ninth century the kings of Wessex had extended their rule as far as the Celtic-settled parts of the south-western peninsula. In the mid-1000s the future King Harold had been leading offensives from Mercia against the Welsh. What was distinctive about this pre-Conquest campaigning, however, was that it was largely confined to the British Isles — even when it took the form of resisting the Viking onslaught. It never involved conflict with the rulers of continental Europe. This extension of activity, when it came, was a result of the events of 1066. England, reduced to satellite status by defeat, was made to serve the interests and ambitions of her new rulers. Her resources were exploited by the sons of William the Conqueror in their struggle to reconstitute the dominions of their father after their separation on his death. Her wealth was tapped to pay for the defence of Normandy against the King of France. Her people groaned under the weight of taxation, as the complaints of the chroniclers testify: tallages were levied every year of Richard I's reign from 1194 to 1198, and the judicial eyre (visitation) of 1194 was said to have drained the realm of wealth from end to end. The loss of Normandy in 1204 and the death of John twelve years later brought a lessening in the intensity of this burden, but not its end. The attempts of John's son Henry III to recover the duchy led to further campaigning and thus to the imposition of further taxation in the 1230s and 1240s. But, with time, the king gradually became reconciled to the duchy's loss and, in 1259, bowing to the inevitable, he signed away his claim to it in the Treaty of Paris. From that moment it was not Normandy on which the continental aspirations of England's rulers were focused, but a duchy much further south — that of Aquitaine.

Aquitaine had come to the Angevin line by the marriage in 1152 of Henry of Anjou to the Aquitanian heiress, Eleanor; it became an English royal domain as a result of Henry's accession to the crown in 1154 on the death of King Stephen. The duchy covered a vast area of south-western France, lacking precise boundaries but stretching roughly from Poitou to the Pyrenees. In the later twelfth century it formed the final link in the long chain of territories that made up the Angevin empire or confederation. But in the thirteenth century, after the loss of Normandy and Anjou, it stood alone, or almost alone, as an isolated dependency, linked by a personal union to the English crown and, after 1254, generally conferred as an apanage on the king's eldest son. The relationship between England and Aquitaine was a very different one from that which had earlier linked England and Normandy. In one sense it was far looser: the two states lay much further apart and they lacked the cohesiveness brought about by the existence of a single ruling class. But in another sense it was a relationship which grew closer over time. The Gascon nobility cherished the autonomy which the rule of an absentee monarch guaranteed them. From their point of view it was far better to have a king (or duke) 500 miles away in London than one only 200 miles away in Paris: their liberties could to that extent be more effectively safeguarded. In addition, it is significant that the two countries' economies complemented each other: Gascony sent England wine and salt, while England sent cereals, cloth and wood in return. The emergence of a wealthy and influential merchant community in Bordeaux went some way to compensate for the absence of a landed tie between England and the duchy.

Through the connection with the duchy of Aquitaine — a connection that was to last until 1453 — England was brought into closer contact with other parts of south-western Europe. The need to secure the duchy's southern frontier encouraged successive rulers to seek alliances, and better relations generally, with the kingdoms to the south of the Pyrenees — Navarre, Aragon and above all Castile. In this spirit, Henry III in 1254 arranged the marriage of his eldest son Edward, the future Edward I, to the Castilian Princess Eleanor. In later times, as Castilian goodwill was undermined by growing French power in the peninsula, the emphasis was placed on seeking support in the most distant of the Iberian kingdoms — but one with which the English shared a similar maritime outlook — that of Portugal. Diplomatic efforts were rewarded in 1386 by the making of a treaty of perpetual alliance between the two kings and their heirs, and it is by virtue of this alliance that Portugal is often regarded today as England's oldest ally.

The growing tensions between England and France in the late thirteenth and early fourteenth centuries and the outbreak in 1337 of the Hundred Years War led successive rulers of these two countries to search widely across Europe for allies — in England's case not only to the Iberian kingdoms but also to Italy and to central Europe. Richard II's marriage in 1382 to Anne of Bohemia, daughter of the Emperor Charles IV, was the result of one particularly ambitious piece of coalition-building; the same king's bid made fifteen years later to win the imperial title may be construed as another (or at least may have been informed by similar objectives). The Anglo-Imperial alliance in the event produced no tangible benefits; nor did the bid for the imperial crown. But the two initiatives should not be written off as embarrassing failures. Each in its own way bore witness to a favourable perception of England's influence in Europe and to the respect in which English military and political power was held. As a result of Edward III's successes in the field, at Crécy for example in 1346, England had moved politically from the fringes of Europe to the centre. England had become a great power; foreign princes regarded election to the Order of the Garter as one of the greatest honours that could be bestowed upon them; and foreign knights eagerly sought employment in English royal service. By the late fifteenth century, of course, the position had been transformed. The English had been expelled from Gascony, and Lancastrian Normandy had collapsed;

great power rivalry thereafter was to be between Valois and Habsburg, not Valois and Plantagenet. But, for a century or two in the late Middle Ages, England was a military power of the first rank in western Europe.

The reality of England's influence in Europe, then, at least in the fourteenth and early fifteenth centuries, was very different from that which its position on the fringes of the medieval cartographer's world might lead us to suppose. The cartographer's view was a theologian's, a cosmographer's, view. It bore little relation to topography; and it bore even less to the world of secular reality. From a theological perspective it is true that England was a kingdom of little importance; it lay far from Rome, and it had only one shrine of the first rank. From an economic or political perspective, however, England's position looked more impressive. She was a country of great wealth which supplied a vital raw material (wool) and which enjoyed trading links with every part of Europe. Her kings were rulers whose continental interests gave her a role in Europe that she had previously lacked and whose ambitions encouraged military organization on a scale never before experienced. Her military power in the late Middle Ages was out of all proportion to her population or size.

The attitude of her people to their neighbours was an amalgam of conflicting ideas and prejudices. The Celtic peoples to the north and west were looked down on after the eleventh century with arrogance and condescension; writers of English birth like William of Malmesbury denounced them as primitive and barbaric. Towards the peoples of continental Europe, however, attitudes were more ambivalent. There was a feeling of inferiority similar to that experienced by John of Salisbury; people were aware by the twelfth century of the greater freedom and liberality to be found in Europe. But increasingly over time there was also a powerful undercurrent of xenophobia, which manifested itself in anti-papalism and hatred of foreigners. In large measure these conflicting sentiments represented stages in the gradual working out of an English national identity. Men who had once seen themselves as either tenants or vassals were now coming to see themselves as belonging to a nation — as sharing a common identity with their fellows. This was a process that was happening not only in England but in France, Scotland and elsewhere. However, in England's case, it was speeded by the loss of the Angevin domains in France. With the Channel once more a frontier, the English were again able to think of themselves as an independent race.

To a greater degree perhaps than was the case with any other medieval kingdom England's relations with her neighbours were determined by the unpredictable fortunes of war. Her colonization by the Vikings strengthened ties with the northern world; her conquest by the Normans led to a reorientation southwards; her search for allies against France brought her into contact with the states of central and south-western Europe. Contemporaries looking at these changes would have been reminded of the image of the wheel of fortune, raising men up and throwing them down again. In sharp contrast to this pattern of mutability, however, were the more stable and long-lasting economic and social ties which linked England and her neighbours. The export and import of goods, and the coming and going of people, kept England in contact with other parts of Europe throughout the Middle Ages, giving rise to cultural interpenetration that was felt by the non-English as well as by the English. The varied character and form of England's ties with her neighbours and the changes that took place in them during the Middle Ages form the subject-matter of the essays that follow.

CHAPTER II

ENGLAND AND THE CONTINENT IN THE ANGLO-SAXON PERIOD

Janet L. Nelson

'SUNDERED TOTALLY FROM THE WHOLE WORLD': thus did a Roman poet see the Britons in the first century BC. Although in the next four centuries Rome's empire expanded to include what are now England, Wales and southern Scotland, the poet's view might have seemed proven right in the fifth century — by AD 500 Rome's power had collapsed and much of England was controlled by Anglo-Saxon immigrants ignorant of the Latin literary culture and the Christianity of the Later Roman Empire. Even in the fifth and sixth centuries, however, there was no real 'sundering': rather, Britain's contacts with the Continent became more varied and complex. The poet's had been a landsman's view and the centre of his mental map was Rome. Instead, we have to see the early medieval world as multi-centred, with Northern Europe not marginal but integral, and the seas around the British Isles not barriers but thoroughfares.

The Anglo-Saxons came from northern Germany and Denmark and the process of settlement in England took a century and more. During this period Anglo-Saxons remained in touch with their homelands and made new contacts too, both with Scandinavia and with the post-Roman Frankish kingdom of northern Gaul. Eastern and southern England thus became part of a zone spanned and unified by the North Sea. Ireland had never been part of the Roman Empire; but, in the fifth and sixth centuries, the Irish adopted Christianity and so were brought into contact with fellow-believers, not just elsewhere in Britain, in Wales and south-west Scotland, but in the Mediterranean world. The Irish Sea, and the wider sea between southern Ireland and Spain, also served to link rather than to divide. Take your vantagepoint, not in Rome, but in England itself, in the fifth or sixth century, and you stand in the centre of a vortex of competing and overlapping influences emanating, directly and indirectly, from many different parts of the Continent. Ideas taken up in England returned thence to the Continent. Whereas Britannia had been on the receiving end of the Roman Empire, contact between England and the Continent in the early Middle Ages meant, in the longer run, exchange.

In the early medieval West, though Rome's complex fiscal and commercial systems had gone, key types of wealth — for reward and for display — were moveable. Plunder was amassed through raiding by land or sea and tribute was exacted, in the form of precious, transportable objects — treasure, valuables, women, slaves and livestock. Archaeologists have been able to reconstruct the communications networks through which some types of objects (notably pottery) were transported; written sources reveal something about exchanges of persons — slave sales and dynastic marriages. Since many valuables were products of areas of northern Europe that could be reached by sea or river, and since transport by boat was relatively cheap and easy, England's place in these networks was not peripheral but central. By the eighth century, the use of coin, lapsed in England since the fifth century, was resumed: the small silver coins, perhaps first put into circulation by traders, were soon issued by kings who were able thus to extract profit as well as prestige precisely because international trade already flourished. English coin promoted exchange between on the one hand, the non-coin-producing societies of the Celtic and Scandinavian north and of eastern Europe beyond the Rhine, and on the other hand, the 'old Roman' Continent that had never lost contact with the southern and eastern shores of the Mediterranean.

Further contacts travelled with raiders and traders. Roman Christianity was borne again into England from several directions: Ireland, Wales and western Scotland; Gaul; Spain; the eastern Mediterranean; and, last but not least, papal Rome whence Pope Gregory I, touched (according to a legend arguably based on fact) by the sight of Anglo-Saxon slave-boys in the market at Rome, in 597 sent his little team of monks to convert the English. Missionaries and church functionaries travelled the length and breadth of Christendom and beyond it. By the eighth century, the Anglo-Saxons had become not only Christians but particularly enthusiastic devotees of St Peter and his (and Gregory's) episcopal successor, the pope. The geography of the Holy City displayed this special relationship: the English settlement in Rome, needed because there were so many English visitors and semi-permanent residents (there is no sign of any Frankish or Spanish quarter), was located right next to the church of St

Peter. To reach 'the threshhold of the Apostle', English people normally crossed the Channel and travelled by land, making strings of contacts en route. The network extended vastly when Anglo-Saxons, notably St Boniface, took on the task of converting the 'Old', or continental, Saxons, whom they believed to be their distant kin. The missionaries sought papal authority, and so routes to and from Rome became still better trodden. There were predictable side-effects: hardly a town between the Alps and Rome, Boniface complained, lacked Anglo-Saxon prostitutes.

By the mid-eighth century, the pope was issuing pronouncements that profoundly affected the everyday lives of Christians: in Gaul on what constituted a valid marriage; in England on distinction of dress and haircut between clergy and laymen; in Germany on whether eating horsemeat was allowed (it was not). These papal pronouncements, incorporated in written collections and widely copied, became church law authoritative over all western Christendom. Among those who did most to transmit this authority, and to spread a unified Christian culture through their own writings too, were Anglo-Saxons. Bede, the Northumbrian, who saw Rome only in his mind's eye, interpreted barbarian history in providential terms that made sense to Franks as well as English; Boniface, the West Saxon, converted Old Saxons and reformed the Franks, while his followers, women as well as men, drew the nobles of central Germany to endow their monastic foundations and present their offspring as prospective monks and nuns; Alcuin, Bede's compatriot, was the teacher of Charlemagne and through him helped to begin the Carolingian Renaissance. It was no coincidence that Boniface and Alcuin, who saw themselves as exiles for God, inspired their own and later generations through letters written home, copies of which were also collected and circulated on the Continent.

In the eighth century, England was divided between several kingdoms. Of these, the most powerful was Mercia, centred in the Midlands, but extending control as far south as the Thames, and overlordship further still, over Kent and Wessex, to reach the south and south-eastern coasts. Though Mercia's 'empire' was small in scale by comparison with the contemporary Carolingian Empire, both depended on the same dynamic: the interests of a warrior aristocracy, the drive to territorial expansion, the quest for plunder and tribute. Charlemagne's reach stretched from the Elbe to the Ebro, and from the North Sea to the Tiber. Offa of Mercia (757–96), however, could worry the pope with threats to intervene (perhaps via the English enclave at Rome) in Roman politics; and when Offa demanded Charlemagne's daughter as a bride for his son, he worried Charlemagne himself. Charlemagne intervened in English politics: he protected *émigré* scholars, notably the Northumbrian Alcuin, a political exile later sent back to England as Charlemagne's trouble-shooter and ecclesiastical diplomat, and also (even more dangerously for Offa) exiles from Northumbria, Mercia's rival, and from Wessex, Mercia's southern client-state. Charlemagne had influence over Scandinavian warbands too: when Vikings attacked the Northumbrian monastery of Lindisfarne in 793 and carried away some of the child-oblates as captives, Alcuin thought Charlemagne might secure the boys' release. After Offa's death (though not before), Charlemagne helped to instal *émigré* princes on the thrones of Northumbria and Wessex; and he acquired the relics of the Northumbrian saint-king Oswald for his imperial relic collection. By the end of his reign, he may well have seen the English kingdoms as in some sense dependencies of his western empire and this notion reappeared at the court of his son Louis the Pious, a keen patron of missions to Scandinavia. The partitioning of Louis's empire after 843 left a legacy of imperial ideology to multiple heirs.

Interpretation of the increasingly complex political, diplomatic and religious contacts between England and the Continent from the mid-ninth to the mid-eleventh century entails an assessment of the Viking impact. In 856, Charlemagne's grandson, the West Frankish king Charles the Bald, exploited the dynastic difficulties of the West Saxon king Æthelwulf (his son had rebelled) to detain him en route home from pilgrimage to Rome and to arrange his marriage to Charles's daughter Judith. Did the kings plan a concerted response to Viking attacks on both Francia and Wessex? Perhaps. But Vikings readily entered the *internal* politics of early medieval kingdoms, whether recruited into the warbands of Frankish and English kings or establishing themselves as settlers both in north/central England and in Frisia (modern Netherlands), where they threatened to draw away aristocratic support from indigenous rulers. Viking warlords showed no reluctance to adopt Christianity. Their power and their work-methods were not so different from an Anglo-Saxon or Frankish king's; but they lacked, as immigrants, their rivals' long-established local roots and dynastic traditions. Charles the Bald strengthened his position at home by assuming the mantle of Charlemagne and was rich enough to buy off, and sometimes recruit, Viking raiders who accepted baptism. When his widowed daughter Judith, on her return to Francia, eloped with Count Baldwin of Flanders

THE HOUSE OF WESSEX IN THE NINTH AND EARLY TENTH CENTURIES
The names of kings are underlined

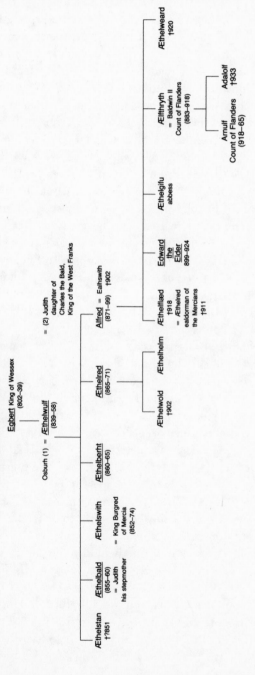

and the couple threatened to seek protection from Roric, the Christian Viking lord of Frisia, Charles responded by accepting both Baldwin and Roric as his faithful men. Later in the ninth century, after Viking warlords had taken control of every English kingdom save Wessex and a truncated Mercia, Æthelwulf's son (and Judith's stepson) Alfred attracted a multinational following to his own court and married one daughter to a Mercian client-ruler, another to the Count of Flanders, the son of Judith and Baldwin — a significant precedent for future exports of English royal women to the continental marriage-market. In arranging the Flemish marriage, Alfred sought, indirectly, to secure his own descent-line in Wessex; after Alfred's death in 899, his nephew, bidding against Alfred's son Edward for the West Saxon throne, would be offered no harbour from Edward's Flemish brother-in-law and so had to seek help from the Northumbrian Danes. Alfred made his court (as Charlemagne had done) a magnet for the ambitious from the Continent as well as from various parts of Britain. Scandinavian rulers in northern England issued coins that imitated Alfred's, thus acknowledging his prestige if not his overlordship. Alfred's enlisting of the Frank Grimbald, former monk of Saint-Bertin and priest of Rheims, proved that he could compete with the most influential of contemporary rulers; and if Alfred could muster at his court Welshmen, Bretons, Scandinavians, Frisians and continental Saxons alongside Grimbald, he could also claim an apostolic patron, Pope Gregory, who outclassed Rheims's St Remigius, apostle of the Franks. The same small, and intensely competitive, political world embraced Wessex and the continental lands linked by the North Sea and the Baltic.

Anglo-continental marriage alliances are a very striking feature of the tenth century. Continental rulers sought Anglo-Saxon royal women for the same reasons — positively, for legitimacy and prestige; negatively, to avoid risks of factional discord inherent in marriage-links with local aristocratic families. The West Frankish King Charles *Simplex* (the Straightforward), as a widower of nearly forty (and after six daughters), anxious not to upset long-laid plans to regain his Carolingian inheritance in Lotharingia, asked Edward the Elder for his daughter as a bride. Charles could not have foreseen that his queen's native land would provide a bolthole for her and their son in 922 when Charles himself was deposed. From Wessex that son would return in 936, with the support of his uncle King Æthelstan, to assume the West Frankish throne. It was probably on this occasion that an Anglo-Saxon royal consecration rite was first used for a West Frankish king. Variant versions of this

THE HOUSE OF WESSEX IN THE TENTH AND ELEVENTH CENTURIES

The names of kings are underlined

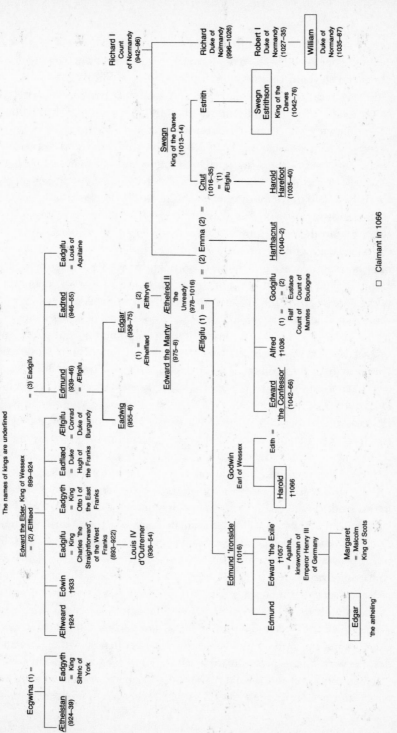

☐ Claimant in 1066

rite — which in the twelfth century (if not sooner) became standard French usage — seem to have found their way across the Channel in the tenth and eleventh centuries, in Anglo-Saxon pontificals.

It was the founder of a new, non-Carolingian, ruling dynasty, the Liudolfing Henry I, king of the Saxons and East Franks, who, in 929, following the West Frankish Carolingian's example of a decade before, sought another of King Edward's daughters (and Æthelstan's half-sisters) as bride for his son Otto, future western emperor. Eadgyth was welcomed, not as granddaughter of Alfred, but as a descendant (so it was believed) of the Northumbrian saint-king Oswald: 'a holy lineage'. Eadgyth brought gifts that may well have been useful in buying off those within the royal family itself who opposed Otto's succession, but the marriage signified no 'Anglo-German' military alliance. Domestic politics, as in the case of Charles the Straightforward, sufficiently explain Henry's choice. Later, Eadgyth's position as Otto's consort made her a possible protectress for St Dunstan when he was attacked by enemies at the West Saxon court: voluntary exile could often be the springboard for a political comeback. From the standpoint of Æthelstan and his successors, diplomatic marriages might misfire. But for the wife-receivers, once a Carolingian had made the first link, intermarriage with the West Saxon dynasty came to signal entrée into a prestigious club: Duke Hugh, son of one king of the rival Robertian dynasty in West Francia, and father of another, also married a half-sister of Æthelstan (securing his agreement by the gift of exceptionally precious relics). Hence, in the 930s and 940s, all three leading dynasties in East and West Francia were interlinked as affinal kin through the West Saxon royal family. It was in a sense their position as outsiders that made Anglo-Saxon brides 'safe' for continental bridegrooms. The marriages did not in themselves show the West Saxon dynasty on a par with the most up-and-coming families of the Carolingian successor-states. And the traffic was all one way: no tenth-century Anglo-Saxon king married a continental bride.

Nevertheless, Æthelstan was gradually drawn into a further series of contacts with the Continent. Some were peaceful: where his father had been prayed for by Breton monks, Æthelstan benefited from the prayers of monasteries 'throughout the whole of Germany'. Other contacts, despite West Saxon preoccupation with conquest and expansion within England, presaged continental military involvement. Æthelstan was god-father and patron of the exiled Breton prince Alan, who recovered his inheritance from the Loire Vikings in 937. In 939, Æthelstan sent ships to Flanders when he heard that his nephew Louis IV was threatened with rebellion 'in maritime parts' and Æthelstan's successor Edmund did the same in 946. Disputes occasioned by the activities of ecclesiastical reformers became enmeshed in politics. Edmund gave a welcome to the (unreformed) community of the Flemish monastery of Saint-Bertin when they objected to a reformer patronized by Count Arnulf of Flanders (932–64). Such Anglo-Saxon intervention provoked Flemish tit-for-tat. In 933, Æthelstan's exiled younger half-brother apparently made for Flanders (which in the tenth century extended as far west as the Pas-de-Calais), but was drowned off the coast. St Dunstan, exiled by Edmund's son Eadwig in 956, stayed until 958 under Arnulf's protection at the reformed monastery of Saint-Peter, Ghent.

English exiles found refuge with more distant continental protectors too: Dunstan's former right-hand man at Liège, while Oswald, nephew of Archbishop Oda of Canterbury and a probable supporter of Eadwig's brother and rival Edgar, went to Saint-Benoît, Fleury and, despite the shortness of his stay (he returned to England as soon as Eadwig was dead, in 958), kept in touch. Peaceful contacts ensued. Texts and inspiration from Fleury fuelled the English reformers later in the tenth century. In the 980s, the Fleury scholar Abbo stayed at Oswald's monastic foundation of Ramsey and there wrote his imaginative account of the martyrdom of the East Anglian King Edmund at the hands of pagan Danes in 871. Copies of Carolingian conciliar decrees entered England to inspire both ecclesiastical and secular legislation. Count Arnulf II (964–88) corresponded with Dunstan and an English nun called Teta gave relics to Saint-Bavo, Ghent.

The extensive power of Edgar (958–75) within England and his aspirations to a Britain-wide authority were reflected in the range and substance of his continental contacts. He wanted Dunstan, already his trusted supporter, to become Archbishop of Canterbury, despite the presence of an existing incumbent: he sent Dunstan to Rome to secure papal approval, at a price, for this uncanonical manoeuvre. In 972, Oswald followed in his footsteps, bearing gifts, after Edgar gave him the archbishopric of York in (strictly uncanonical) addition to the see of Worcester. Edgar had already been in contact with the German court of Otto I and exchanged rich gifts. And again there were more general links with German monasteries via personal and spiritual connections: through these, for instance, the Old High German poem *Heliand* reached

England. Edgar's idea of a 'British' empire, with its distinctive Irish Sea orientation, was probably inspired by Ottonian example. While Edgar's envoys were at Otto's court for Christmas 972, Oswald, it seems, returned from Rome with papal blessing for the 'imperial' coronation of Edgar at Bath in 973. The royal emissaries had displayed their master's wealth and prestige to the rest of Christendom. No wonder Edgar's court exerted its own centripetal pull: 'he attracted foreigners and enticed harmful people to this country', wrote Archbishop Wulfstan of York, late in the reign of Æthelred II, when the Continent contacted England with a vengeance. Edgar's attractive power could be seen in hindsight to have had unfortunate consequences.

Why did Vikings concentrate their attacks on England in Æthelred's reign rather than, as in the ninth century, on Flanders or the lands around the Lower Seine? The Flemish counts' diplomatic skills or the Norman dukes' part-Viking ancestry would surely have counted for little had a new generation of Vikings not found a source of more plentiful, and sounder, money in England: a source, moreover, which thanks to centralized royal control of coin issue was easy to tap. In the late tenth and early eleventh centuries Scandinavians came for cash and the frequently encountered peckmarks on coins in Scandinavian hoards show a shrewd preference for sound money. How had so much silver been accumulated in the England of Æthelred II? Æthelred's fourth code, of c. 1000, which is concerned with tolls taken at London, mentions traders coming from Normandy, Flanders, West Francia, Lotharingia and Germany. Pepper was imported from the east, probably via Venice and Mainz. How were the imports paid for? Sales of English wool abroad may already have been bringing in German silver from the Ottonian Reich, slaves were a valuable export and re-export, and the English government and its associates (such as the Archbishop of Canterbury) may simply have been very good at creaming off the wealth of England. By contrast, though Flemish towns were multiplying and thriving on trade, few had mints and money was in short supply. In the late tenth century several Flemish monasteries seem to have depended on successive archbishops of Canterbury for gifts, presumably including money. It was no wonder that the Scandinavians focused their attention on England.

What was Æthelred to do? His papally underwritten agreement with Duke Richard I of Normandy in 991 was probably not about mutual defence but about ecclesiastical politics, specifically the disputed succession to the archbishopric of Rheims — hence papal concern. In the

990s, Æthelred saw the main Scandinavian threat coming from the north and west, via Norse settlements in Ireland and the Isle of Man, and he focused his military response there. But, as the century turned, the south and south-east began to seem more vulnerable. That perception surely lay behind Æthelred's initiative in seeking a closer alliance with Duke Richard II, whose sister Emma he married in 1002. It was soon after this, however, that Æthelred sent ships to attack Scandinavians in the Cotentin peninsula. Probably the Norman duke, based in Rouen, had little control in the Cotentin; but it looks as if he, and the Count of Flanders too, were happy to deal with Scandinavians at Æthelred's expense. As attacks became more concentrated and co-ordinated, Æthelred tried to employ traditional tactics against the Danish King Swegn: he backed the return to Norway of an *émigré* pretender and, in 1012, detached the Danish warlord Thorkell from Swegn and recruited him into his own service. But the tax levied to pay Thorkell's men undermined Æthelred's already shaky position in his own kingdom and he was forced to seek refuge with his brother-in-law in Normandy (though his adult sons by an earlier marriage remained in England). It is possible that Duke Richard had already entered some kind of alliance with Swegn who, by 1013, had clearly decided on a total conquest of Æthelred's kingdom. Swegn's sudden death early in 1014 caused Duke Richard to reconsider: Æthelred's return was negotiated, nominally through Edward, his ten-year-old son by Emma and hence Richard's nephew. Within two years, however, Æthelred was dead and soon his eldest surviving son, King Edmund 'Ironside', was dead too. One of Swegn's two sons, Cnut, who had married an Englishwoman (the daughter of an ealdorman of York murdered at Æthelred's behest in 1006), became, by conquest, King of England. Significantly, there is little sign of 'national' opposition to a 'foreign' take-over: just as Thorkell had joined Æthelred and married an Englishwoman, so the Mercian ealdorman Eadric joined Cnut. A thread of Mercian–West Saxon hostility runs through the tangled politics of 1015–16; and the inhabitants of eastern and northern England were markedly more ready than the southern English to co-operate with Scandinavian overlords. Cnut established his regime in part by appropriating native traditions that underlined English divisions and at the same time defamed Æthelred. He commemorated Æthelred's half-brother King Edward the Martyr, murdered in 979, allegedly with the connivance of Æthelred's mother. Cnut also commemorated Archbishop Ælfheah of Canterbury, killed in 1012 while resisting taxation which

Æthelred had ordered to pay Thorkell's men. Cnut presented himself as breaking with Æthelred's tyrannical government. Marriage was a key act of conciliation, signifying union between Danes and English and in 1017 Cnut (apparently without repudiating his English first wife) married Æthelred's widow, Emma. Æthelred's two sons by Emma had fled to Normandy, and Cnut's new marriage was also intended to head off Norman intervention on their behalf. Through Emma, Cnut thus re-formed Æthelred's Norman alliance. Edmund Ironside's two sons threatened intervention from elsewhere: too young to lodge a claim in 1016–17, they found refuge at the court of the German Emperor Henry II. It was the existence of these Anglo-Saxon *æthelings* (kings' sons) on the Continent, as well as the continental dimension of Cnut's own rule, that made the English kingdom the focus of continental ambitions from several quarters in the eleventh century.

On his own brother's death in 1019, Cnut returned to Denmark, and the rest of his reign spanned the two kingdoms. A permanent fleet had to be maintained, out of taxation, to operate an empire linked by the North Sea. Cnut spent most of his time out of England. Favoured Danes tended to be rewarded in Denmark rather than in England, for Cnut could bolster his English government by recruiting local 'new men' (notably Godwin), whereas his position in Denmark was under recurrent threat from Scandinavian rivals and from German border-raids. A coalition of those hostile powers with Danish rebels shook Cnut's regime badly in 1026: hence Cnut's appearance at Rome for the coronation of Emperor Conrad II in 1027 to assure future imperial non-interference; and hence too Cnut's letter to his English subjects promising to rule 'justly and faithfully from now on'. Chickens began to come home to roost when the new Norman Duke Robert (1027–35) threatened attack on the exiled *æthelings*' behalf.

When Cnut died in 1035, there were four contenders for the English throne: Harold Harefoot, Cnut's son by his first, English, wife, and Harthacnut, Cnut's son by Emma; also Emma's two sons by Æthelred, Edward and Alfred. Since Harthacnut had already been set up as king in Denmark and hence would maintain an Anglo-Danish empire run on English tax-revenue, many English nobles preferred Harold Harefoot, who promised a regime separate from Denmark. Emma masterminded a division of England's rule between Cnut's sons, but only one of those sons was *hers* and, when his cause began to fail in England, Emma summoned from Normandy her two older sons by Æthelred. Within weeks, the *ætheling* Alfred was murdered and his brother Edward retreated to Normandy. In 1037, Emma herself was driven to take refuge in Flanders. Her successive schemes had been scuppered by lack of Norman support: her nephew Duke Robert died in 1037 in Asia Minor while on pilgrimage to Jerusalem and, during the minority of her little great-nephew William, Normandy's internal conflicts precluded any exploitation of the situation across the Channel. Coincidentally, Count Baldwin IV of Flanders also died in 1037, and Baldwin V, though able to accommodate Emma in style at Bruges, was in no position to intervene in England. Emma did not give up. By 1039, her son Harthacnut was secure enough in Denmark to bring a fleet to Bruges and their invasion of England was forestalled only by Harold Harefoot's death in 1040. An English delegation reached Bruges to acknowledge Harthacnut as king. Once in England, he signalled the re-creation of his father's Anglo-Danish empire by levying 'a very severe tax' to pay off part of his fleet. Emma's hand can be seen in further continental involvements. The *ætheling* Edward was summoned again from Normandy in 1041 and associated in his half-brother's rule to bolster the legitimacy of an increasingly unpopular regime. When Harthacnut died in 1042, Edward succeeded him. One reason for a ten-month delay before his consecration, in 1043, may have been his desire to secure the approval of the German Emperor Henry III, who sent envoys bearing gifts to witness the ceremony. Edward's nephew and namesake remained in Henry's protection and was soon to be married to one of Henry's kinswomen. Disputes between rival, and frequently short-lived, rulers, and a consequent series of exiled royals on the Continent, had created complex continental interests in the English succession.

Edward's reign saw an intensification of continental contacts — some dangerous, as when Baldwin V of Flanders harboured a series of pro-Danish exiles in the 1040s; others benign, as when Edward recruited the Norman Robert to be Archbishop of Canterbury or sent the Lotharingian Hermann, Bishop of Ramsbury, to attend Pope Leo IX's reform council at Rome in 1050. In 1054 Edward sent Bishop Ealdred of Worcester to the court of Emperor Henry III. Through such visits, the latest liturgical books, and models of ecclesiastical reform, were brought to England. When Emma, and later Edward the Confessor's widow Edith, wanted propagandistic writing produced for them, both turned to Flemish monks. Edward was following Cnut's example when he granted land in England (in both cases including land at a Kentish port) to a

Norman monastery (Cnut to Fécamp, Edward to Mont-Saint-Michel). One of Edward's motives in encouraging such a range of continental connections was to keep open the question of the succession (as Elizabeth I was to do) and so give himself room for manoeuvre.

In an age of Continent-wide economic expansion and growing competition for the wealth to back political authority, the English kingdom, with its exceptional concentration of royal resources, including control of a large and high-quality coinage, appeared to an increasing number of interested continental parties a very valuable prize — and an attainable one. Eustace, Count of Boulogne, visited England in 1051 and married Edward's widowed sister Godgifu. By that date, Edward and his queen, Edith, daughter of the powerful Earl Godwin, had been married five years without producing any children. One of Edward's intentions in repudiating Edith in 1051 and exiling her kinsmen may well have been to remarry. Meanwhile, his link with Eustace would help to protect the Kentish coast from Scandinavian fleets. Edward was not the only one to seek a cross-Channel alliance: Tostig, son of Godwin, married the daughter of the Count of Flanders, perhaps in 1051. When Godwin and his family were exiled later that year, they went to Flanders. Duke William of Normandy, too, visited England in 1051, perhaps hoping to pick up some of the forfeited lands of Godwin's exiled sons.

In 1052, Edward recalled Godwin to favour, and Edith to his court — but perhaps not (if rumour was true) to his bed. The succession remained a pressing issue. Although there were princes immediately across the Channel, Edward's thoughts turned to his long-lost kinsmen who had found refuge in the German Empire over thirty years before. He was unsure of the exact whereabouts of the *ætheling* Edward, son of Edmund Ironside, and his children: Bishop Ealdred, sent to Cologne in search of them, was told that they were in Hungary. Thence, in 1057, they returned to England bearing rich treasures (and perhaps leaving behind a pontifical containing the Anglo-Saxon coronation liturgy). But the *ætheling* died soon after. His daughter Margaret stayed at King Edward's court: in 1067 she fled to Scotland, married the King of Scots, applied Hungarian missionary methods and was eventually canonized. The *ætheling*'s son, Edgar, was officially named *ætheling* by King Edward: unlike his father, however, Edgar was not a king's son.

In 1065, others set their sights on Edward's throne. At the bottom of that year's crisis lay the continental alliance of one particular magnate: Godwin's son, Tostig, the Flemish count's son-in-law, quarrelled with his brother Harold and, exiled by King Edward, naturally sought refuge in Flanders. Harold (who had succeeded to his father's earldom in 1053) needed continental allies against his brother and set sail for northern France, probably making for Boulogne. He was shipwrecked on the coast of Ponthieu and handed over to William of Normandy. The claim of post-1066 apologists that Edward had sent Harold to promise William the succession seems contradicted by the admission of those same apologists that Harold's presence in Normandy was an accident. More likely, the sequence was the reverse: realizing that William himself had designs on the English throne, Harold conceived a bid of his own — a decision later stiffened by Scandinavian intervention. William, driven by political weakness in Normandy to seek new resources, was lucky to get his expeditionary force across the Channel, still luckier to win the English throne. The conquest of England — a much harder task than it had been for Cnut — was to occupy the rest of William's reign.

The political history of the later Anglo-Saxon period is incomprehensible without its continental context, but Anglo-Saxon England itself is part of that context — of northern Europe and of Christendom. Because England was European, Anglo-Saxon bishops could travel to Rome and to the Rhineland and speak the language of ecclesiastical reform. Because England was European, Anglo-Saxon magnates could visit the courts of northern Europe and speak the language of oath-taking and chivalry. Because England was European, Anglo-Saxon traders could operate in ports on the Seine and the Rhine (and Cnut at Rome could discuss their protection from burdensome tolls), just as their opposite numbers could operate on the Thames. Successive eleventh-century conquests incorporated England in continental states: they were able to do so only because political sundering was offset by more profound forms of belonging.

CHAPTER III

THE NORMAN CONQUEST

R. Allen Brown

OF ALL SUBJECTS IN ENGLISH HISTORY the Norman Conquest must surely be the most controversial, which is a pity. At bottom one may feel the problem to be less academic and more a matter of lingering national prejudice, combined with insularity, not so very different from that which inspired Edward Augustus Freeman to write his great Victorian *Norman Conquest* over a century ago, the six volumes of which (1867–79) still have much influence upon those who have not read them.

Though, often enough, woolly minds with bogus scholarship pretend it is not so, we do have sufficient evidence to know most of what happened, why it happened and with what result. The answers are usually in favour of the Normans, but are unacceptable to the Anglo-Saxons who are numerous among us, and not only on the Clapham omnibus. Identifying with the real Anglo-Saxons (or were they Anglo-Scandinavians?) as 'Us', and therefore 'Right', they resent the Normans as 'Them' and therefore 'Wrong'. One may begin with a passionate plea that an appreciation of, even admiration for, Old English achievement, should not lead to a denigration of the Norman.

Freeman really did see the Norman Conquest in terms of clean-limbed Englishmen, all liberals and at least potential members of the Church of England, done down at Hastings by dirty foreigners, using dirty tricks (e.g. cavalry and archers) and aided by the Scarlet Woman of Rome. To him that defeat was unendurable and so he comforted himself and his readers by claiming that it was only temporary, everything coming right in the end. He wrote (and note the use of the personal pronoun throughout) that England gained 'not so much by anything which our Norman conquerors brought with them, as through our own stores which it was an indirect result of the Conquest to preserve to us', so that 'in a few generations we led captive our conquerors; England was England once again, and the descendants of the Norman invaders were found to be amongst the truest of Englishmen.' The rich culture, traditions and institutions of pre-Conquest England would turn the conquerors into such heroes of the Victorian constitution as the barons of Magna Carta, Simon de Montfort and Edward I. Meanwhile, it was Freeman, of course, who also set Earl Godwin of Wessex and Earl Harold his son in their improbable roles of national and patriotic heroes.

Among modern professional historians, the approach is more sophisticated, though not always as much so as one might hope. (The phrase 'Norman thugs' hissed round the room at a graduate seminar I once attended in London — though admittedly on that occasion hostility to the Normans was partly provoked by their failure to promote the cause of Women's Lib.) More responsibly, the burgeoning of Old English studies in our time seems both to lead to a veneration of all things Anglo-Saxon admitting of no criticism of any kind, and to combine with the fashionable historiographical trend for continuity, at all costs and times, which diminishes the impact of the Conquest upon English history more effectively than ever Freeman was able to do. That all is not well in this matter, and that modern scholarship has not greatly altered underlying attitudes since Freeman's day, may perhaps be shown by two quotations from established and distinguished historians. The first comes from *The Governance of Mediaeval England* by H. G. Richardson and G. O. Sayles:

> For half a century or so from 1066 the English way of life was not sensibly altered. The Normans had very little to teach, even in the art of war, and they had very much to learn. They were barbarians who were becoming conscious of their insufficiency.

This is both polemical and irresponsible, yet, if it unnervingly echoes Freeman on the one hand, it also echoes F. M. Stenton on the other. The latter's *Anglo-Saxon England*, first published in 1943, is still the Bible of Old English studies, and rightly so. The penultimate sentences of that great work read as follows:

> The Normans who entered into the English inheritance were a harsh and violent race. They were the closest of all western peoples to the barbarian strain in the continental order. They had produced little in art or learning, and nothing in literature, that could be set beside the work of Englishmen.

Though Sir Frank Stenton then added his final sentence, 'But politically, they were the masters of their world', every other statement in that memorable passage is at fault, either explicitly or implicitly.

It helps to bring the Norman Conquest into focus if it is first set in its proper, and anything but insular, context. It was, after all, only one incident in the amazing Norman expansion of the age, which is a fundamental feature of Norman history. 'Norman expansion began as it went on, its origins were the origins of Normandy itself' (John Le Patourel, *The Norman Empire*). The Normans began with the creation of Normandy from very small beginnings as an inchoate Norse settlement in northern France in *c.* 911 (i.e. the official date of the so-called Treaty of Saint-Clair-sur-Epte, whereby Rollo's Seine Vikings were granted uncertain territory around Rouen, the details and even the date of which are lost). About the year 1000, individual Norman knights began to be involved in the politics and warfare of southern Italy in Capua and Apulia, with the result that by about 1060 the whole of Italy south of Rome was under Norman domination, and by 1091 the whole of Sicily also — in an adventure story even more remarkable than the take-over of England in the same century. In 1063, three years before the invasion of England, Normandy's southern neighbour, the county of Maine, was absorbed into Norman lordship. From England, of course, the Normans penetrated deep into Wales and Scotland, as they were to penetrate Ireland in the twelfth century. Meanwhile, at the close of the eleventh century, the Normans broke out of the confines of Latin Christendom altogether when they became the leaders of the First Crusade (two Norman armies, from Normandy and from Norman Italy, under Robert Curthose and Bohemond of Hauteville respectively) and founders of another Norman principality at Antioch in northern Syria. Individual Norman participation in the wars against the Infidel in Spain and audacious Norman attacks from Italy against Byzantium herself also took place. Evidently, there was nothing insular about the Normans, whatever may be the case with some of their latter-day historians, and the Norman Conquest of England is better seen as an event in European history than as an incident in English history. Furthermore, this physical expansion was only one item of a total Norman achievement which extended from spirituality, monasticism and statecraft to warfare, via learning and the arts. There was nothing philistine about the Normans either, as their churches from Durham to Monreale and beyond testify.

It also helps to get what we call the Norman Conquest of England into focus if we realize that it was not meant to happen as it did, and that Hastings, which distorts our view of it into an affair of blood and iron, was not a long-term intention. The means and methods of Norman expansion were almost everywhere the same — aristocratic penetration and settlement, infiltration and involvement in local politics, marriage, the creation and vindication of claims, the exercise of ecclesiastical patronage and the planting of churches and castles as centres of influence and power, thus imposing lordship. All this was backed up by a military capacity that could seem invincible. Violence rode with piety, as on crusade.

For the most part, it is a story of long-term take-over, rather than sudden and arbitrary conquest. Antioch as the result of the First Crusade, and Sicily with the element of Holy War, may have been a little different, but not very. Certainly it is not a tale of folk-migration or the crushing in arms of one nation by another. Indeed, Norman peasants or humble parish priests are never mentioned, only lords and would-be lords and knights, abbots and monks, who take over the levers of power and the rich agricultural land. Thus it was in the creation of Normandy itself, thus it was in the piecemeal imposition of Norman lordship upon southern Italy, thus it was in the absorption of Maine, and thus it was also in the matter of England in the sixty years or so before 1066. But in England there was opposition, more potent than elsewhere and very nearly successful: an opposition not national or Churchillian in the spirit of 1940, but directed by the house of Godwin, contrary to the wishes of the king himself, against an increasing Norman influence rightly seen as a threat to its own dominance in the realm. Hence, as a last resort, Harold Godwinson's seizure of the throne, and hence Hastings.

The Norman 'Conquest' thus began not in 1066 but, as indeed Freeman saw, in 1002, with the marriage of Æthelred II to Emma of Normandy, daughter of the duke, Richard I — though even before that the histories of Normandy and England were becoming interlocked by Viking raids and settlements in both. The first issue of that marriage was the future Edward the Confessor, half Norman from the start, and a kinsman in due course of the future Conqueror.

From now on it is necessary to rehearse certain reported events, almost all of which are controversial. The difficulty is that most of the evidence concerning the preliminaries of the Norman Conquest and the rights and wrongs of the disputed succession of 1066 comes from Norman sources, chiefly William of Poitiers, William of Jumièges and the Bayeux tapestry. The Old English sources, such as they are — chiefly the Anglo-Saxon Chronicle and the *Vita Edwardi* — are ambiguous or enigmatic or simply silent about the things that matter most. The objection is made that the chief Norman sources are selective and biased, and accordingly of little value; and it is true that they raise their problems. But it is not open to discount any and every piece of evidence from the Norman side which does not fit one's own more prejudiced hypothesis on the ground that it emanates from something anachronistically thought of as The Official Norman Version of Events, a tissue of lies and propaganda. In fact, the Norman version of events cannot be disproved by the usual methods of historical scholarship and tends to be confirmed by independent evidence. It also fits the wider context of all that is known about the history of the Normans, Normandy, England and the eleventh century.

In 1013, in the course of the conquest of England by Swein Forkbeard of Denmark, we know that Æthelred sent Emma and their children to Normandy for safe refuge. There, at the Norman court, Edward the Confessor was to remain for some twenty-eight years until his return in 1041 to become king in 1042. Born about 1005, he was some eight years old when he left England, and thus spent not just his youth (as is often said) but also the prime of his manhood in Normandy. Moreover, at least during the reign of Duke Robert the Magnificent (1027–35 and the Conqueror's father), who is thought to have become the sworn-brother, Scandinavian-fashion, of Edward and his younger brother Alfred, the Confessor was evidently the official Norman candidate for the disputed English throne. He appears with the title of 'king' in Norman charters, and Duke Robert even mounted an expedition against England on behalf of him and his brother Alfred, which was only prevented from sailing by the weather. The date was c. 1033–4 and the incident an eerie anticipation of the eventual Norman invasion of 1066. Alfred himself visited England in 1036 on some mission of which we know little, save that it was connected with the succession, and was murdered on the orders of the then king, Harold Harefoot, at the hands of Earl Godwin. There is no reason to suppose that Edward the Confessor ever forgave Godwin and his house for the murder of his brother, and it is certain that the Normans never allowed it to be forgotten. Indeed, they regarded Hastings as, among other things, a due punishment upon Harold, Earl Godwin's son: 'For the sins of the father shall be visited upon the children', and the eleventh century is an Old Testament age.

Next, when Edward did return to England in 1041 to become king somewhat improbably in 1042 — with Norman assistance, according to Norman sources, and by the influence of Earl Godwin the Kingmaker, according to English sources — he felt obliged, or was obliged, to marry

Earl Godwin's daughter, Edith. The political pattern of the intended continuing dominance of the house of Godwin can surely be deduced: the marriage has the appearance of being loveless, was certainly childless, and so itself leads on to 1066. But Edward also brought with him certain Norman friends, as the English sources abundantly testify, as well as those Norman sympathies and preferences which the Norman sources claim; the former he appointed, as was natural for a king, to high places in the state. Chief among them was his particular friend Robert 'Champart', Abbot of Jumièges, who threatened to cut out Earl Godwin and his sons at court. Edward created him firstly Bishop of London and then, in 1051, and to the fury of the Godwin faction, Archbishop of Canterbury. By now there was a veritable Norman colony in Herefordshire on the Welsh border under Earl Ralf, King Edward's 'foreign' nephew from Mantes in the Vexin, adjoining Normandy, and another, it seems, in Essex. In both areas the new and alien French and Norman lords raised castles, the first to be seen in England and the particular instruments of Norman colonization and expansion:

> The foreigners then had built a castle in Herefordshire in Earl Swein's province [thus the outraged Anglo-Saxon Chronicle: Earl Swein was one of Godwin's many sons] and had inflicted every possible injury and insult upon the king's men in those parts.

There can really be no doubt that the rebellion of Earl Godwin and his sons in 1051 was occasioned not merely by increasing Norman penetration of the realm but by Edward's promise of the succession to his young kinsman William, the future Conqueror, in that year. To establish William's recognition as heir by the English magnates, hostages were taken, significantly from Earl Godwin to ensure his lasting compliance. The Norman sources (details in William of Poitiers) insist on these events, and, if they occurred, 1051 is certainly the date for them. King Edward won the first round: Godwin and his sons were exiled; Edith, his daughter and Edward's queen, was packed off to a nunnery at Wherwell, and two of our native sources refer, enigmatically as ever, to an unexplained and highly unusual visit by the Norman duke to England in the following year. But the second round went to the Godwinsons who, in 1052, were back again, in arms, and by *force majeure* were reinstated, evidently on their own terms: Edith was brought back to court and most of Edward's Norman friends were driven from the kingdom, including Robert of Jumièges. (Hence the subsequent scandal of Stigand, a clerk and creature of the Godwinson faction, who was uncanonically made Archbishop of Canterbury in Robert's place, even while retaining the bishopric of Winchester which he already held.)

Presumably the renewed Godwinson ascendancy explains the recall to England in 1057 of the *ætheling* Edward, son of Edmund Ironside (the son of Æthelred and Ælgifu his first wife) to be made heir, though nothing came of this because of his immediate death in circumstances thought suspicious by the Anglo-Saxon Chronicle. The next relevant fact in the so-called Norman version of events, which has every appearance of being true, is the mission of Earl Harold, the son and heir of Godwin, to Normandy at a date most likely to be 1064. Harold, the Norman sources tell us (the English sources say nothing at all), was sent by King Edward to confirm the earlier promise of the throne to William, and, in William of Poitiers's detailed account of a famous occasion, not only did this but swore to aid the duke's succession, did homage to him to become his man, and then received investiture of all his lands in England. In some accounts Harold was also offered a daughter of the duke as wife. Thus, in Norman eyes, when Harold seized the throne himself on 6 January 1066, the very day of Edward's funeral, he stood revealed not only as a usurper but a perjuror, and Hastings became inevitable as the inexorable judgement of God: 'Shout unto God with the voice of triumph, for the Lord most high is terrible' (Psalm XLVII: 1 and 2).

It is not the purpose of this chapter to interpret either Harold's actions or his motives but rather to explain the Norman Conquest as a classic exercise in Norman expansion and enterprise. Nevertheless, it seems unlikely that his *coup d'état* in January 1066 was long premeditated or could have been foreseen. In Normandy in 1064, he had evidently found it necessary to support the Norman cause and had done his best by fealty, homage and investiture to safeguard his own position in the now likely event of a Norman succession. Thereafter he must have thought, rightly, and like Godwin in 1051, that that position would be untenable in the circumstances of Norman lordship, and have been carried away by the drama attending the Confessor's death, the old king's alleged death-bed bequest of the kingdom to him, and his election or recognition by the magnates then in London.

These facts, including the tangled politics of the England of King Edward's day (about which, in the immortal words of the Anglo-Saxon Chronicle, 'it is tedious to relate fully how things went'), may bring the so-called Norman Conquest of 1066 into proper focus. They may also

help to explain how it came about that, after careful diplomatic prepara-
tion (to which Harold made no response), Duke William of Normandy
invaded England in September 1066 with the support or acquiescence of
official opinion in Latin Christendom and, above all, with the blessing of
the papacy. It is easy to imagine how that last fact infuriated the
Protestant prejudice of Freeman and his compatriots, but it is more
important to realize that it meant the backing of the foremost moral
authority of the time, itself of much more consequence than the backing
of the United Nations today.

The modern controversy about the Norman Conquest is, however,
concerned at least as much about results as about the rights and wrongs
of 1066. The issue here is continuity or change. In reality, the changes
were profound and took place right across the board. 'Sooner or later,'
as Stenton wrote, 'every aspect of English life was changed by the
Norman Conquest.' Nor could it be otherwise in an age of personal
kingship and personal lordship, since the Conquest brought, whatever
else, and quite beyond dispute, a complete change of personnel at the top
in a new and alien ruling dynasty and ruling class in Church and State.
That change subsumes all others, including the reorientation of England
in the affairs of Latin Christendom which immediately followed and
which is the main theme of this article. Another important theme is the
growing connection between England and Normandy before 1066 and as
from 1002.

Apart from this association, the closest affiliations of pre-Conquest
England in the eleventh century were beyond question with Scandinavia,
to the point where Anglo-Scandinavian rather than Anglo-Saxon may
seem the better term to apply to it. All England had been conquered by
Swein Forkbeard and Cnut, his son, some fifty years before the Norman
Conquest, and four Danish kings sat in turn upon the English throne,
Swein, Cnut the Great, Harold Harefoot and Harthacnut. Inevitably,
they created a partly new and largely Anglo-Scandinavian aristocracy. In
language and writing at least, the Scandinavian earl (*jarl*) replaces the
Anglo-Saxon ealdorman and the housecarl replaces the thegn. Godwin
himself, though English, was a creature of Cnut. He was given the
earldom of Wessex, extending from Cornwall to Kent and containing the
heartlands of the Wessex monarchy itself, and was married to Gytha, a
Danish princess, the sister of Cnut's brother-in-law. Four of their six
sons were given Danish names: Swein, Gyrth, Tostig and Harold himself.
The Danish court and clientage in England was added to the Danish

settlement and the Danelaw of Alfred's day and after. Harold Hardrada of Norway as well as Duke William of Normandy landed in England in 1066 in a bid for the English throne and, when he did so, the men of York, the city of the former Norse kingdom of Eric Bloodaxe, joined him after the battle of Gate Fulford and offered to march with him against the south.

The great age of the Viking world was ending by the mid-eleventh century, and what had been its English province was giving rather than receiving (Cnut painstakingly becoming the Christian king; English missionaries going to Scandinavia). There was no future in Scandinavia or in Germany and the Rhineland where England also had close connections. Flanders may have been *sui generis* because of its trade and industry, but Germany, the kingdom of the East Franks, was, like England, a surviving sub-Carolingian society, and the future lay with northern France. Old-fashioned is the best, and most inoffensive, epithet to apply to pre-Conquest England, in everything from warfare to the Church. It is irresistible to add that in 1066 at Hastings the Old World went down before the New (as at Civitate in far-off southern Italy in 1053, the crack but obsolescent Swabian infantry had gone down before the heavy cavalry of Norman knights). The Norman Conquest wrested England from the barren Scandinavian world and largely replaced the ties with Germany by others far closer of its own. After 1066, D. C. Douglas's 'conjoint realm' (*William the Conqueror*) and John Le Patourel's 'Norman Empire' (*The Norman Empire*) became the reality. Under far-flung Norman management, the English kingdom became automatically a potent unit in contemporary European politics, was brought to the centre of the stage and, more particularly, was associated with northern France, whence came so much of that medieval civilization of which the twentieth-century West is still the heir.

At the merely political level, Sir Richard Southern wrote, in a lecture meaningfully entitled 'England's first entry into Europe' (Creighton Lecture 1966, printed in *Medieval Humanism*) that 'the Continental connection dominated English government throughout the twelfth century', as it did long afterwards. As from 1066, the kings of England and their magnates who were their vassals had at least one foot in northern France and their horizons were wider yet. The Angevin prince, our Henry II, Count of Anjou, King of England, Duke of Normandy and Aquitaine, who succeeded the Norman monarchs upon the throne in 1154, bestrode his world, which was not narrow, like a Colossus; and so did his sons, especially Richard I, the Lionheart. Continental interests and ambitions led to wars in, and subsequently against, France, which lasted until 1815 and in men's minds beyond. If war is the catalyst of change, this matters very much. In fact, the wars between France and England are fundamental to the history of both. In England, the strains and stresses and the endless demands for supplies led straight from the Domesday Book to the Magna Carta. Edward I was constrained to reissue and confirm John's Great Charter because of his wars in France. Edward III, that paragon of medieval princes, victor of Crécy (and Poitiers through his son the Black Prince), founded the Order of the Garter and rebuilt Windsor Castle as its headquarters out of the spoils of war. Richard II was brought down at least partly because he made peace with France. Henry V's fame rests upon his French campaigns and his victory at Agincourt. Mary, in the sixteenth century, still had Calais written on her heart.

Moreover, England (itself pressing hard by influence as well as in arms against Wales, the lowlands of Scotland and Ireland) was in these centuries, as the direct result of the Norman Conquest, a French province. As from 1066 in England the ruling class, and presumably the almost innumerable dependants of their households, spoke French, while the universal Latin of western Europe which was Latin Christendom replaced the precocious vernacular of Old English as the language of learning, liturgy and administration. The Domesday Book, which has sometimes been attributed to Old English know-how by those who also seek to make Hastings an English victory, was written in Latin, and so (after about 1070) was that wildly over-praised but (before 1066) most rare of Old English instruments, the vernacular sealed-writ. King William used, and carried on the building of, Edward the Confessor's palace of Westminster, as he used and extended the Old English royal palace at Winchester, but all over England he and his lords and vassals raised castles as the means of occupation and also as the expression of a new and feudal lordship. William the Conqueror's Tower of London and the chapel of St John within it stand as a symbol of the new, because augmented, regality of the Norman successors to the Old English throne.

All over England great churches were built or rebuilt for the greater glory of God and as a manifestation of that reform of the English Church which the Normans undoubtedly saw themselves as accomplishing. They were also, no less than the castles, an expression of new lordship, ecclesiastical and lay. Every major church was rebuilt within a generation or two of the Norman Conquest, save only the Confessor's Westminster, which was a Norman church already, and Harold's Waltham Holy Cross, which was presumably politically untouchable until Henry II rebuilt it over a century later. These churches tell a tale beyond piety and aesthetics. They were built upon the Norman model, but even bigger. Scale as well as austerity were the marks of *Normanitas* (Jumièges, Mont-Saint-Michel, St Stephen's at Caen in Normandy; Winchester, Durham, St Albans, Bury St Edmunds in England) and 'imperial' is the adjective to apply to Norman building (cf. the British in India). Here and there one finds 'English' features, which prove nothing except that the Normans were the most eclectic of peoples, owing as much in their achievement to immigration as to emigration, adopting and adapting whatever they found and liked, and so building in Norman Italy churches which to us do not look Norman at all (most notably the Capella Palatina at Palermo). 'After their coming,' wrote William of Malmesbury (an early twelfth-century historian usually praised for his balanced judgement, except when he criticizes Anglo-Saxon England), 'they revived the rule of religion which had there grown lifeless. You might see great churches rise in every village, and, in the towns and cities, monasteries built after a style unknown before.' The English Church no less than State was under Norman management after 1066, and so became part of a wider world. While under Lanfranc's guidance (Lanfranc, a Norman from Pavia in northern Italy), leading Norman monasteries like Bec, St Stephen's (in Caen) and Fécamp sent monks to run the Church of England, others like St Evroul sent out their sons to southern Italy and Sicily, where the new Norman lords were allies, not only of the papacy but also of Monte Cassino, the prestigious fount of Benedictine monasticism. [I don't know if the British Parliament is still the best club in the world, but in the late eleventh century the Norman old-school tie was certainly the best.]

Everything of consequence in England, and in English life, was changed in the aftermath of the Norman Conquest. It is true that in the opinion of some historians the business of government is an exception: English government, it is argued, had long been more efficient than the Norman, and the Normans, in this area, had little to teach, and much to learn from the English. Certainly, we can agree that the Normans made few alterations to the structures that they took over from the English. More important to the argument, however, is the way in which those structures were used; and in the light of recent research there can be little doubt that the Normans not only made them run more efficiently but also turned them to new purposes. The Domesday Book, that most striking early monument to bureaucratic efficiency, was accomplished in Norman and not in Anglo-Saxon England. When we contemplate the enormous effort that went into the making of this survey, we can begin to understand why Thomas Carlyle could write, 'Without them [the Normans], what had it ever been?'

CHAPTER IV

THE NORMAN WORLD
OF ART

Deborah Kahn

THE VICTORY OF DUKE WILLIAM OF NORMANDY and his army in 1066
cleared the way for an invasion into England of artistic fashions
which were already firmly established on the Continent. But even in the
pre-Conquest period England was not entirely cut off from the artistic
life of the duchy. During the peaceful reign of Edward the Confessor
Norman culture and art had already begun to infiltrate. Edward was
himself half Norman and had spent much of his early life in Normandy;
upon receiving the English crown in 1042, he naturally enough surrounded
himself with Norman advisers and maintained certain Norman customs.

A pious man, Edward had been deeply impressed by monastic reforms
carried out in Normandy by William of Volpiano, formerly Abbot of
Saint-Bénigne at Dijon. This, too, had important consequences for
England. At the time of the Conquest there were some twenty-eight
monasteries in Normandy; among the most important were those at Bec,
Bernay, Jumièges, Mont-Saint-Michel and Saint-Ouen at Rouen. These
houses, some old foundations, others newly established, were built in the
monumental early Romanesque style. It was according to the mould of
such buildings that Edward the Confessor began the work which was to
occupy him for the rest of his life, Westminster Abbey.

The plan of the abbey drew directly upon the early Romanesque style
then current in Normandy. It is particularly close to that of Jumièges
Abbey which was being rebuilt at about the same time (1040–67) and on
the same grand scale. The church at Westminster was even built of Caen
stone, a pale, fine-grained limestone imported from Normandy, which
became one of England's principal building stones after the Conquest.

But the influence was not just one way: certain Anglo-Saxon trends
influenced the arts in Normandy. Anglo-Saxon manuscripts were much
admired on the Continent for their vibrant colours and expressive,
vigorous style. Late Anglo-Saxon manuscript illumination itself was

ultimately based on Carolingian models; the famous masterpiece of the Rheims School, the Utrecht Psalter (c. 816–35) had been in Christ Church, Canterbury, since c. 1000, where it was copied several times during the eleventh and twelfth centuries. The first copy, the Harley Psalter (of the early eleventh century), faithfully imitates not only the iconography of the Utrecht Psalter, but also its lively, sketchy drawing. Anglo-Saxon draughtsmen absorbed this style and elaborated on it, making it their own. With it they produced fine line or wash drawings and illuminations rich in pinks and blues with a lavish use of gold. Another characteristic of these paintings was the profuse use of exuberant acanthus foliage painted in elaborate, interwoven border patterns around full-page illuminations. This style was dominant in major *scriptoria* across southern England, at Glastonbury, Canterbury, Winchester, Ely and Ramsey, but it is known as the Winchester School style because of the large number of manuscripts which survive from there.

The so-called Winchester School style had a strong influence on Norman painting and, to a lesser degree, on sculpture. The abbey of Jumièges played an important part in the diffusion of the style in Normandy. One of its abbots, Robert, appointed by Edward the Confessor first to the bishopric of London in 1044 and later in 1051 to the archbishopric of Canterbury, made rich gifts of Anglo-Saxon manuscripts to Jumièges. Although clearly not an isolated instance of such contact, it is of particular interest because manuscript illumination, stone and ivory carving at Jumièges all show Anglo-Saxon influence.

There were of course other artistic traditions in England. Scandinavian art gained great popularity, especially during the rule of the Danish king, Cnut (1016–35). The 'Ringerike' style, which evolved towards the end of the tenth century, usually includes an animal motif, the Great Beast, interwoven with snakes and slender plant tendrils to form a dynamic pattern. An example of this style, which was executed in England and has an impressive composition, vigour and tension of form, is the relief from a sarcophagus found in the churchyard of Old St Paul's Cathedral in London. It has a runic inscription on one edge, while the front is carved with the type of motif described above.

Anglo-Saxon artists excelled not only as sculptors and illuminators of books, but as embroiderers, metal-workers and ivory carvers. Of these rich treasures only a pitiful fraction survives; but much information about them can be gleaned from documentary sources. Among the recorded treasures which belonged to King Edward was a ship with a golden lion on the stern and a golden, winged dragon on the prow. Some idea of the splendour of such works, produced on the eve of the Conquest, may be obtained from the golden bookcover of a Gospel book of Countess Judith of Flanders, wife of Tostig, Earl of Northumbria. It depicts Christ in Majesty surrounded by cherubs, and Christ on the Cross flanked by the Virgin and St John. The craftsmanship and material is of the highest quality: embossed gold, filigree, precious stones, pearls and translucent *cloisonné* enamels. No contemporary examples of textiles survive, but again documentary references to them are numerous. Their fame was such that when Eadmer, monk and historian of Canterbury, accompanied Archbishop Anselm to Bari in the late eleventh century, he was shown vestments which Cnut's queen, Emma, had sent from England to Benevento.

None of these artistic traditions died out with the Conquest, but following the political events of 1066 new patrons took control in England and their demands on artists and craftsmen were different from those of the Anglo-Saxons. Duke William placed Norman and other northern French barons in all the major seats of power — as earls and sheriffs, bishops and abbots. The primary concern of the duke and his men was how to maintain military and administrative control in their new country. Architecture became an important tool to meet that end and dramatically new building styles were introduced.

It is significant that the Conqueror's first action on reaching English shores was to construct an earth-and-timber castle. After the Conquest, a network of castles was rapidly built at strategic points across the country. The two major keeps erected by the Conqueror survive, one at Colchester, the other in London. Both are massive, austere structures and it is only too easy to imagine how they must have daunted and intimidated the newly conquered Anglo-Saxon population who, it must be remembered, had no previous tradition of castle building. Great keeps or *donjons* were usually tower-like structures, built on artificial earth mounds. They provided living quarters for the lord and his men, a prison in the depths of the basement and a stronghold system with surrounding defences. This type of arrangement remained important during the reign of Henry I, as the mighty example at Castle Hedingham illustrates.

Even more important as a means of controlling the local population was the Church. In the decades immediately after the Conquest, the Church undertook a prodigious amount of building. Before 1066, churches in Normandy were of moderate size, but in newly conquered

England wealth was available which encouraged architecture on a truly grand scale.

Anglo-Saxon monasteries and cathedrals were considered by the Normans as old-fashioned and were soon demolished and replaced with large Romanesque buildings, in the first instance based on the type which had evolved in Normandy and thereby continuing the trend which had already begun with the building of Westminster Abbey. These buildings can generally be characterized as consisting of a three-apsed or ambulatory plan, with wide, sometimes aisled transepts, a crossing tower, a nave with aisles and often two massive western towers. The internal elevation, generally three-tiered (aisles, galleries, clerestories), had such massive walls that passages were often threaded through their thickness. The interiors were articulated with regular repetitive units: columns, capitals and simple mouldings.

Durham Cathedral is one of the outstanding examples of the type of building erected in England after the Conquest. It is dramatically situated on high ground, with a river below, its twin tower façade dominating the massive rock on which it was built. The sombre interior is memorable for the alternating system of round columns incised with geometric patterns and compound piers. Durham Cathedral is important for technical as well as aesthetic reasons. The building, started in 1093 and consecrated in 1133, was rib-vaulted in stone throughout. The introduction of rib-vaulting at Durham opened the way for great architectural advance: the rib reinforced the weak point of the vault and allowed substantial developments in quadripartite and sexpartite vaulting to be made in Normandy and in England.

With the reorganization of the Church in the years after 1066, monastic life blossomed and a range of intellectual activities was encouraged. Two successive archbishops of Canterbury, Lanfranc and Anselm, Italians by birth, but both trained at the powerful Norman abbey of Bec, were scholars of European reputation who helped to shape the revival of English intellectual life. Both scholars were more interested in the texts of books than in their illustration.

Nevertheless, there were changes in manuscript illumination after the Conquest. The sumptuous service and devotional books and Bibles of the pre-Conquest period, often with magnificent full-page illuminations, were to a large extent replaced by the type of illumination current in the duchy. In Norman manuscripts, ornament was chiefly confined to initials. These were often inhabited by men or monsters, or enriched with foliage. The humans and grotesques were sometimes involved in a violent struggle, with occasional detail of specific events, mainly from the Gospels. But narrative cycles, in manuscript illumination at least, were only revived c. 1120–30 in such manuscripts as the St Albans Psalter, now in Hildesheim, or in certain related works such as the *Life and Miracles of St Edmund*, from the once enormous and powerful monastery at Bury St Edmunds, and now in the Pierpont Morgan Library in New York.

Secular narrative art, on the other hand, flourished after the Conquest. One of the greatest works of this period, the Bayeux tapestry, is an epic document of the events leading up to the Conquest. There is now fairly conclusive evidence that the tapestry (in fact an embroidery) was commissioned in Canterbury by Bishop Odo of Bayeux, the half-brother of the Conqueror. The work consists of six linen strips embroidered with woollen thread of rich, earth-tone colours. The main events are flanked by delightful borders abounding in humorous anecdotal detail. The original function of the tapestry is not entirely clear. It has been argued that it was a hanging for Bishop Odo's castle or that it was made for the choir of Bayeux Cathedral, to be displayed on certain ceremonial occasions. But sadly there is no strong evidence to settle the issue one way or the other.

The original use of the tapestry raised the interesting question of the interior decoration of buildings. Here the Conquest is unlikely to have had any great effect, for buildings in England and Normandy were apparently decorated in much the same way. Weavings or embroideries were sometimes used to enliven the wall surface but even in the eleventh century almost all church interiors would have been decorated with wall-paintings, as demonstrated by those in the rural church of St Mary, Ickleton (Cambridgeshire).

Sculpture was also used in the decoration of many buildings, both inside and outside; here too there were marked contrasts in the Anglo-Saxon and Norman approach. Sculpture in Anglo-Saxon England was generally applied to buildings in a rather haphazard way and carvings were placed at random on wall surfaces. One of the strengths of the Norman sculptural tradition was its intimate connection with architecture. Another fundamental difference between the two sculptural traditions was the type of capital used in Normandy and in England. At the time of the Conquest, the most popular form of capital in the duchy was the Corinthian capital with angle volutes (scrolls). These were also occasionally employed in England, but the most usual English capital form was the cushion or cubic type. Such capitals appear to have reached England from Flanders or Germany, possibly even before the Conquest, but seem to have been unknown in Normandy. Even after the Conquest, when artistic links between England and Normandy were at their closest, cushion capitals were never much used in the duchy. The capital provided an ideal surface for painting, but marvellous sculptures were also adapted to fill it. The charming examples in the crypt of Canterbury Cathedral, with dragons and other monsters crouching in the shield of a cushion, show what great imagination was used by the artists responsible.

In some cases, particularly immediately after the Conquest, Norman carvings in England were indistinguishable from those of the duchy. The capitals in the crypt of Gloucester Cathedral, or in the castle chapel at Durham, with masks and volutes, and geometric backgrounds, are very similar to examples at the abbey of La Trinité at Caen or at Graville-Saint-Honorine.

However, native Anglo-Saxon sculptors also continued to find employment. Their productions, both those which perpetuate old styles and those which attempt to imitate new Norman fashions, are usually designated Saxo-Norman overlap work. The church of St Mary at Sompting in Sussex, for instance, with capitals on which the volutes are transformed into animal horn shapes enclosing berries, provides a clear instance of the naïve adaptation of Norman forms by Anglo-Saxon carvers.

The victory of the Anglo-Norman style in England was assured, and yet the traditions of Anglo-Saxon art were not completely eclipsed. The legacy of Scandinavian art long remained influential. One of the most telling instances of this is the capital of c. 1130 from the cloister (now destroyed) at Norwich Cathedral. Its decoration consists of two wingless dragons on each face, intertwined together, their snake-like tails terminating in foliage tendrils. A Viking-age brooch found at Pitney in Suffolk is so similar that one could almost imagine it as the model for the capital. Anglo-Saxon art, particularly works in the Winchester School style, also continued to inspire artistic productions of the late eleventh and twelfth centuries. The charming tympanum of the humble parish church of St Mary at Halford in Warwickshire is carved with a three-quarter angel holding a scroll. The proportions of the figure, in addition to such features as the trailing drapery flourishes on the sleeves, are extremely close to certain late Anglo-Saxon illuminations. Winchester School style acanthus continued to be used as well; one of the cushion capitals in the crypt of Canterbury is carved with lush acanthus, as are several metal and ivory pieces, also from Canterbury. Anglo-Saxon models continued to be used, even in the second half of the twelfth century; the roundels at Malmesbury Abbey, for instance, were based on Anglo-Saxon prototypes.

The Norman Conquest transformed Anglo-Scandinavian England into an Anglo-Norman nation and with that transformation the Romanesque style took root. One can argue that even had the Conquest never occurred, Anglo-Saxon art would eventually have given way to the Romanesque style, but the process would probably have been much slower. In the event, it was the Norman Conquest which led England to join the artistic life of mainland Europe.

CHAPTER V

THE MONASTIC REVIVAL

Hugh Lawrence

WHEN THE NORMANS ARRIVED IN ENGLAND, monasteries had long been a feature of the social landscape. Thirty-five houses of Benedictine monks appear in the Domesday Survey as possessing land in the time of Edward the Confessor, and there existed upwards of nine nunneries. Many of these abbeys were endowed with great estates. A few of them, like Bury St Edmunds which had been founded by Cnut, were still relatively young establishments in 1066; but most of them traced their continuous history from the monastic revival inspired by Dunstan and Æthelwold a century earlier.

We do not really know much about the observance of the abbeys and cathedral monasteries in the last decades of Anglo-Saxon England. The childhood recollections of Eadmer, the Canterbury monk who became chaplain and biographer of St Anselm, and Ordericus Vitalis, dispatched from England as a tearful child of ten to be a monk at Saint-Évroul, suggest an easy-going affluent lifestyle in some of the pre-Conquest houses. But both men wrote long afterwards and their view of the past was coloured by their subsequent experience. The English monasteries housed aristocratic communities and the abbots known to us were drawn from the high nobility. As cult centres of the Old English saints, they were the foci of national sentiment and traditionalist in their interests. However, there are indications that their observances were not as insular as some have thought. At any rate, their liturgical routine cannot have differed very much from that of the French and German monasteries, for it was still determined by the *Regularis Concordia* — the body of common usages agreed by the English monks in 970 and modelled on the practices of Fleury and Ghent. Nevertheless, they displayed none of the spiritual dynamism that characterized the new monasticism of the Norman duchy; and they were apparently indifferent to the currents of thought and learning that were transforming the intellectual world of the eleventh century.

They were now subjected to the invigorating shock of a Norman take-over. The revival of monastic life in the duchy of Normandy had begun in the year 1001, when the Italian ascetic William of Volpiano brought a party of monks from Dijon to restore Benedictine observance at Fécamp. William came at the invitation of Duke Richard II, and under ducal and baronial patronage the revival was extended to other houses. The ancient abbeys of Jumièges, Saint-Wandrille and Mont-Saint-Michel were re-peopled with monks. And there were new foundations, among them the abbey of Bec started by Herluin, the convert knight, in 1034, and St Stephen's at Caen, founded by Duke William himself only a few years before the invasion of England. It was from these centres of young and dynamic monastic life that the Conqueror recruited a new race of abbots who were gradually installed in the English monasteries. Many of them came accompanied by groups of French monks from their own com-munities. Lanfranc, when he was brought from ruling St Stephen's, Caen, to take up the archbishopric of Canterbury in 1070, imported a number of monks from Caen and Bec to join the community of Christ Church, Canterbury, including a fellow Italian, Henry of Bec, whom in due course he appointed prior of the cathedral monastery.

This alien invasion was obviously deeply disturbing for English monks, who had to accommodate themselves to a new superior and brethren whose language they could not understand. Tension in the cloister was often heightened by the scant respect that the new abbots showed for English customs and for the Old English saints. Lanfranc purged the calendar of Christ Church of all but a handful of Saxon names. At St Alban's his nephew, Paul of Caen, contemptuously demolished the tombs of his Saxon predecessors to make way for new building. The same happened at St Augustine's, Canterbury, where Abbot Scotland, who had come from Mont-Saint-Michel, had the entire complex of churches constructed by his predecessors levelled to the ground. The bitterness and sense of disorientation caused by this insensitive treatment found expression in various ways. At Christ Church it was reported that an English monk had suddenly gone mad. Elsewhere, at St Augustine's and Glastonbury, resentment erupted into violence.

Besides infusing new blood into existing monasteries, the Conquest was followed by new foundations, for which the patrons imported monks from France. The most conspicuous of these was the Conqueror's own foundation at Battle — St Martin de Bello — built, in fulfilment of a vow, upon the site of King Harold's last stand at Hastings, and peopled by monks from Marmoutier in the Touraine. On a smaller scale, several Norman lords established priories of a modest size adjacent to the castle which was their major residence and the administrative centre of their barony, and persuaded monks from home to occupy them. The monks were the spiritual counterpart of the knights who garrisoned the castle. Priory and castle jointly formed a unit of alien colonization in a hostile land. One of the most influential of these creations was the Cluniac priory founded by Earl William de Warenne at Lewes in Sussex.

Several of the greater French abbeys had received gifts of land and churches in England from the grateful conquerors; but they showed little enthusiasm for setting up dependent houses in a territory they regarded as barbarous and unfriendly. St Hugh of Cluny refused a request from King William to send monks for English abbeys on the grounds that supervision of a distant overseas dependency would be impossible. But Hugh's reluctance was eventually overcome by the persistence of William de Warenne. William and his English countess, Gundrada, had visited Cluny and been deeply impressed; and on returning home they determined to create a Cluniac priory near the earl's castle at Lewes. For this purpose William donated the newly built church of Lewes and an endowment big enough to support twelve monks. Hugh at first demurred, but in the end he was induced to send a prior and three monks to start the foundation.

At the end of the eleventh century under the regime of St Hugh, Cluny was entering on its greatest period of expansion, and the priory of St Pancras at Lewes proved to be only the first of thirty-six houses which came to constitute the English province of the Cluniac empire. They formed one of the most enduring links with the monastic world of the Continent. Lewes, which was the largest and richest — in the thirteenth century its numbers fluctuated between fifty and fifty-five monks — came to have a privileged rank in the order. Its priors, appointed by the Abbot of Cluny and usually drawn from the mother-house, were often men of distinction. One of them, Hugh of Anjou, followed his uncle as Abbot of Cluny in 1199 and left his mark on the order by inaugurating the system of annual general chapters.

In some long-established communities, the Norman take-over, and the destruction of much that was familiar and cherished, awoke a quickened interest in the Old English past. One of the consequences of this was a revival of monastic life in the North, which had vanished in the course of the Danish occupation of the ninth century. Inspired by the cult of St

Cuthbert and Bede's account of the early Northumbrian saints, Aldwin, the Prior of Winchcombe, and two monks from Evesham set out for the North in 1073–4 with the purpose of settling on the derelict sites of Wearmouth and Jarrow. The enterprise prospered. It attracted support from the northern baronage and the Norman bishops of Durham, and led within a few years to the refoundation of Whitby Abbey and new foundations at Selby and St Mary's, York. The most eager promoter was William of St Carilef, the Bishop of Durham. Himself a monk from Maine, he appreciated the English tradition of monastic cathedral chapters and in 1083 he brought monks from Wearmouth and Jarrow to serve the cathedral of Durham and assume custody of the shrine of St Cuthbert. Like most of the new prelates imported from France, William was an energetic builder. His most durable monument is the massive cathedral he began erecting on the hill above the River Wear, which is one of the supreme masterpieces of Norman Romanesque. Its dramatic site and proximity to the castle bear eloquent witness to the complementary role of monks and knights in the Norman settlement of England.

It was a mixture of piety and policy that moved the king and the new military aristocracy to donate part of their property to monasteries. The primary motive, stated in innumerable charters, was that of safeguarding the souls of the benefactor and his family. To found and endow a community of monks was to ensure for the benefactor a perpetual fund of intercession and merit which would avail him and his relatives, both during life and after death. It was an act that rendered satisfaction for the sins of the donor. The penitentials, with their elaborate schedule of penances, inculcated in medieval people a conviction that satisfaction in the form of penance must be rendered to God for sin. One of the graver sins was homicide, even if the killing was that of an enemy in legitimate warfare. The victors of Hastings were reminded of this by a papal legate, Bishop Ermenfrid, who visited England in 1070 and prescribed penances for those who had fought, with the significant proviso:

> Anyone who does not know the number of those he wounded or killed must, at the discretion of his bishop, do penance for one day in each week for the remainder of his life; or, if he can, let him redeem his sin by perpetual alms, either by building or by endowing a church.

Penance could be commuted for specific acts of charity; foremost among these was material support to churches and to monks, who were *ex professo* the 'poor of Christ'. It was this that moved many Norman settlers to donate land to their monasteries at home and in some cases to endow new foundations in England.

Besides piety, there were considerations of social convenience and public policy. The practice of child oblation, authorized by the Rule of St Benedict, made monasteries convenient homes for the surplus children of the landed classes and professional families — for those sons who could not be provided with an adequate inheritance, or daughters for whom no suitable marriage alliance could be found. Until the twelfth century, when opinion veered against it, children donated by their parents were a major source of recruitment to the Benedictine houses. But alongside family strategy, there was the question of public good. The rulers of society who gave property to monasteries expected temporal as well as spiritual returns from their investment. The abbeys and priories of Norman England, ruled and peopled by monks from France, were vital centres of loyalty to the new regime. As corporate landlords with powers of seignorial and, in some cases, of public jurisdiction, they were effectively the governors of wide territories, just as their Saxon predecessors had been. Now, under the new dispensation, the heads of the older abbeys became tenants of the Crown, required to supply quotas of knights for the royal host or the garrison of royal castles in return for their lands. This obligation of abbots and bishops to provide knight service, which had existed in France and Germany since Carolingian times, was introduced into England by the Conqueror.

The Norman influx breathed fresh intellectual life into the English monasteries. With the new abbots came the books and learning of the Continent. They also brought the customs and liturgical usages of Norman monasticism which were derived from the practice of Cluny. The constitutions Lanfranc gave to Canterbury Cathedral Priory, which were widely copied elsewhere in England, reproduced the Cluniac customary with only minor amendments. They ordained a pattern of community life, largely inherited from the Carolingian past, in which liturgical prayer enriched by elaborate ritual was the major task of the monk and occupied the greater part of his day. The manual labour commended by St Benedict's Rule had been squeezed out of the timetable. A proportion of any monastic community was occupied in the managerial tasks involved in running great estates but domestic work was done by hired servants.

By the end of the eleventh century, this traditional form of monastic life was coming under pressure from new and disturbing forces. Monastic leadership in the world of learning was being challenged by the rising schools of the seculars in northern France and northern Italy. The age of the *magistri* — the secular masters — had begun. Within the monastic world itself, accepted notions of the monk's vocation were being called in question by new ascetic movements expressing dissatisfaction with the prevailing version of the Benedictine life. The reaction was partly a protest against the wealth and worldly involvement of the great abbeys; partly a rejection of a regime that imposed a crushing burden of communal prayer and liturgical ritual, and made no concession to the need of the individual for solitude, private prayer or reflection. In their quest for disengagement, simplicity and solitude, the leaders of the movement, like the Gregorian Reformers, drew their inspiration from what they believed to be the order of the primitive Church. Their thinking focused upon three models suggested by Christian antiquity, and each provided inspiration for new forms of religious life.

The first was the example of the desert anchorites of Egypt and Palestine, made known through the *Lives of the Fathers* and the *Conferences* of Cassian. In the eleventh century, the lure of the desert again became a major factor in Western religious experience. The ideal of the eremitical life inspired groups of hermits who congregated in the mountain regions of central Italy and in the forests of Burgundy and Maine; it also found institutional expression in new religious orders of an austere kind. The earliest of these, which began with the founding of the hermitage of Camaldoli in the Tuscan hills by St Romuald, never penetrated England. But two other eremitical orders — the Order of Grandmont founded by Stephen of Muret and the Carthusian Order, which sprang from St Bruno's foundation of the Grande Chartreuse — made their appearance on the English scene in the course of the twelfth century.

Another fertile source of inspiration for new religious institutions was the idea of the apostolic life, the manner of life, that is, of the Apostles as described in Chapter 2 of *Acts*. To the leaders of the Gregorian Reform movement of the eleventh century, the essence of this appeared to be life in community, based upon the renunciation of marriage and personal property. Hildebrand and St Peter Damian urged that this style of life was proper to the secular clergy, who exercised the apostolic role in the Church. In response to this propaganda, houses of canons regular began to appear in the eleventh century in France, Italy and Germany. These were communities of clergy, in some cases cathedral chapters, who had renounced personal property and adopted a fully monastic regime of common dormitory, refectory and choral offices. They were a hybrid order of clerical monks. In the course of the twelfth century, they adopted the so-called Rule of St Augustine as their identity card — an exhortatory treatise on the monastic virtues, which had originated as a letter addressed by Augustine to a community of nuns. This, being much less detailed than the Rule of St Benedict, left each establishment latitude to devise its own regime. The Augustinian canons regular were not really an order, for although some of the greater houses like Saint-Victor at Paris and Arrouaise established dependencies, the majority of priories were autonomous and followed their own customary without reference to any overriding organization. Thanks to enthusiastic promotion by bishops of the reforming tendency and lay patrons, the number of canons regular increased rapidly in the last decades of the eleventh century.

The same search for a primitive model of the religious life moved other groups to press for a more literal observance of the Benedictine Rule. They demanded greater seclusion from the outside world, a reduction in liturgical ritual and a restoration of manual work to the monk's timetable. Out of these discontents and initiatives developed new orders — those of Tiron, Vallombrosa, Savigny and Cîteaux — all dedicated to reviving what was believed to be the original observance of the Rule. Generally, the leaders provided the inspiration, and it fell to their successors to translate the charisma into new institutions. The Cistercians, for instance, originated in the withdrawal of a group of monks from the abbey of Molesme, led by their abbot, Robert, in 1098. All they sought was seclusion and poverty, and their settlement at Cîteaux in the Burgundian forest was hardly more than an obscure hermitage until the arrival of St Bernard with thirty recruits in 1112. In the following three years, the community sent colonies to La Ferté, Pontigny and Clairvaux, and the institution entered an era of meteoric expansion.

St Bernard was the foremost apologist and recruiting officer for the order; and although he was not the founder, its austere observance and passionate propaganda bore the impress of his dominant personality. A novel feature of the Cistercians, made necessary by their initial refusal to accept serfs or the customary sources of manorial income, was their use on a scale hitherto unknown of *conversi* — illiterate lay-brothers recruited largely from the peasantry — as a labour force on their estates. But in the sense that it represented a more literal interpretation of St Benedict's Rule, the Cistercian observance was unoriginal. What was new was the articulated constitution of the order which, as it evolved, was set out in an updated text of the *Carta Caritatis*, the foundation manifesto attributed in its original form to Stephen Harding. The outcome of this evolution was a closely co-ordinated federal structure. Every abbey was made responsible for supervising its own daughter houses; all abbots were required to assemble every year at Cîteaux in a general chapter, which was the supreme governing body of the order.

The newly forged territorial and cultural links with France meant that England was fully open to the rising tide of religious innovation from the Continent. The canons regular made their appearance in England before the end of the eleventh century. Possibly the earliest foundation was St Mary's, Huntingdon, which owed its foundation to Eustace, the Norman sheriff. But a close second was a community of clergy at St Botolph's, Colchester, who decided to adopt a monastic regime and borrowed the customs of the canons of St Quentin at Beauvais. During the twelfth century, the enthusiastic patronage of the Anglo-Norman baronage promoted many new foundations of canons. In fact, numbered by their houses, they came to be the largest order in the country.

There were several reasons for this success. The label of Augustinian canon covered a diversity of observance and a wide variety of establishments. The canons were to be found not only in priories great and small, but also serving hospitals, communities of nuns, the chapels of baronial castles and, in the case of Carlisle, a cathedral church. Their versatility and the possibility of founding a religious house with only a handful of clergy and a correspondingly modest endowment made them attractive to the lay patron of moderate means, as well as to parsimonious princes. The canons thus found patrons among men of the ministerial class, like Henry I's minister, Geoffrey de Clinton, who founded Kenilworth Priory, and Ranulf Glanvill, the founder of Butley and Leiston priories in Suffolk.

Butley and Leiston represented two different forms of canonical life. The former was a house of black canons, who followed a moderate monastic regime and were not averse to accepting pastoral responsibilities. The latter belonged to the more austere order of white canons, the Premonstratensians, who traced their origin from St Norbert's hermitage of Prémontré and modelled their observance on that of the Cistercians. Like the Cistercians too, they sought to avoid secular involvement and chose secluded sites for their settlements. Many of their houses were quite modest in size; so they appealed, like the black canons, to middling landowners anxious to reap the spiritual rewards of founding an ascetic community. It was a minor baron of Lincolnshire, Peter of Goxhill, who brought them to England in 1143 to people his foundation of Newhouse. By the end of the century, twenty-seven houses had been founded in England.

The most conspicuous conquest made by the new monasticism was that of the Cistercians. They were preceded by a few years by the austere Norman order of Savigny, which supplied monks for the abbey of Furness, founded by Stephen of Blois. But from the 1130s onwards, it was the white monks of Cîteaux, with their ascetic reputation and their aggressive revivalist claims — in St Bernard's phase, 'the restorers of lost religion' — who excited the greatest interest and attracted the most enthusiastic support of the military aristocracy in France and England. The first plantation was made at Waverley in Surrey in 1128; the monks were brought from L'Aumône through the offices of William Giffard, the Bishop of Winchester. But the greatest impact was made by a community sent from Clairvaux by St Bernard at the request of a Yorkshire baron, Walter L'Espec of Helmsley, in 1132, to found a new abbey at Rievaulx. By the end of the year, the example of the monks of Rievaulx had persuaded a group of dissidents from St Mary's, York, to seek admission to the Cistercian order; their settlement in Skelldale formed the nucleus of Fountains Abbey. Rievaulx proved to be the harbinger of a wave of Cistercian settlement in the north of England.

Although they were representatives of a French order, the white monks quickly established themselves as an integral feature of the English social landscape. Their activities as cultivators of wastelands — the consequence of their preference for secluded sites — and large-scale producers of wool constitute a well-known chapter of English economic history. The native element was strong from the outset. There were Yorkshire men at Clairvaux in St Bernard's time, who formed the nucleus of the party that was sent to settle at Rievaulx. The order quickly recruited among the Anglo-Norman nobility and also, with spectacular success, among the English peasantry, who supplied the *conversi*. Ailred of Rievaulx's biographer tells us that in 1167 Rievaulx contained 140 choir monks and 500 lay-brothers. Waverley in the 1180s housed 70 choir monks and 120 lay-brothers. What preserved the international dimension of the order were the constitutional links between English abbeys and their founding houses overseas, and annual journeys of English abbots to the general chapter, where they met continental brethren and brought back news and instructions from abroad. These meetings were the only regular form of international assembly known to medieval Europe.

The winds of ascetic revival from across the Channel touched women as well as men. The aristocratic order of Fontevrault owed its English plantation directly to the French connection, for Fontevrault was the chosen mausoleum of the Angevin dynasty, and it was Henry II who introduced the order to England. It represented a form of monastic life long since vanished — the double monastery, consisting of a nunnery ruled by an abbess and served by an adjoining community of monks. The order had only three houses in England, but it probably provided the inspiration for the only exclusively English religious order to be created at this period. This was St Gilbert's order of Sempringham. Gilbert founded the first houses to meet the religious needs of women, for whom the new orders made little provision. He planned to affiliate them to the Cistercians but, when his petition was rebuffed by the general chapter, he adopted something resembling the Fontevrault plan and created double monasteries of nuns served by communities of Augustinian canons. By the end of the twelfth century, Gilbert's order contained nine double houses and four for canons alone, all of them in England, with a heavy concentration in his native Lincolnshire.

The colonization by the new orders reflected the fact that England was an integral part of Latin Christendom. The process was materially assisted by kings with great continental dominions and a French-speaking aristocracy, who continued to look to France for their religious and cultural standards as well as their manners. But in the monastic world, as in secular society, a process of mutual assimilation or 'aculturation' was taking place. The Benedictine houses continued to receive abbots from French monasteries under the Norman kings, but the succession of aliens tailed off after the middle of the twelfth century. The new orders, after the initial plantation, quickly recruited heads, as well as members, of English or Anglo-Norman birth. By the end of the century, monastic communities were normally bi-lingual in French and English. In the Benedictine abbeys, while a native tradition visually reasserted itself in the great schools of manuscript painting at Winchester, Canterbury and Bury St Edmunds, the products of their *scriptoria* and the contents of their libraries show that the monks shared with their overseas brethren a literary culture that was common to western Christendom.

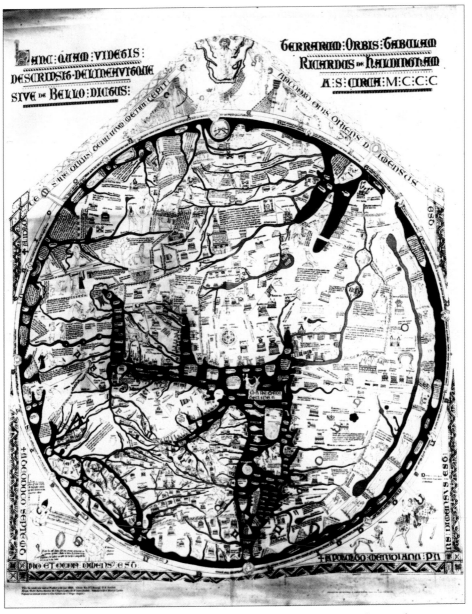

1 The Hereford Cathedral world map, c. 1277–89. The British Isles are shown on the left-hand side of the lower semi-circle.

2 European monarchs: the Danish Cnut and the Norman Emma, King and Queen of the English, present a cross to the New Minster, Winchester.

3 The chapel of St John in the Tower of London, the construction of which dates from c. 1080.

4 'Mere English' or Anglo-Scandinavian? Harold swearing oaths of fealty to William of Normandy, c. 1064 (from the Bayeux tapestry).

*5, 6 & 7 Variation and decoration: the nave of Durham Cathedral (above);
capitals from Canterbury Cathedral (above right) and St Mary's, Sompting (below
right). These details testify to the continuing influence of Anglo-Saxon and
Scandinavian traditions.*

8 Cover from the Gospels of Judith of Flanders (c. 1060). The splendour of craftsmanship and material testifies to the vitality of English art on the eve of the Conquest.

9 Fountains Abbey, founded in 1132, a flagship of the early Cistercian settlement of northern England.

10 Tomb of Henry II at Fontevrault Abbey, France.

11 Geoffrey of Anjou (from his tomb in Le Mans Cathedral); his marriage to Matilda in 1128 was to safeguard her rights in England and Normandy.

CHAPTER VI

THE ANGEVIN EMPIRE

Richard Benjamin

IN DECEMBER 1154, A YOUNG MAN by the name of Henry was crowned King of England. Although only twenty-one, he was already an experienced ruler. At sixteen, he had become Duke of Normandy. Two years later his father, Count Geoffrey of Anjou, had died and Henry succeeded him. The following year, he became Duke of Aquitaine when he married Eleanor, the heiress to the duchy. A duke twice over, he now added king to his many titles. This vast empire, stretching from the highlands of Scotland to the Pyrenees was passed on intact to his son Richard the Lionheart, and then to Richard's younger brother John.

For fifty years, until John lost most of his continental lands to the French king in 1204, England was only one of many lands ruled over by a family from Anjou. Small wonder that Henry II and Richard I spent less time in England than their later medieval successors. Yet English historians have often been less than sympathetic to the demands made by such an 'empire'.

> For an absent King
> Is bound to bring
> His Kingdom care
> If he's never there

wrote Eleanor Farjohn in her verse on Richard I for school children in 1932. Of course, this assumes that England was for some reason more important than the lands in France, as well it might appear to an Englishman. But the Angevins were not Englishmen: they were the French-speaking rulers of most of France.

The counts of Anjou had begun as minor castellans in the Loire valley. Around the time that their lords, the Capetian dukes of France, promoted themselves to kings, the house of Anjou decided to follow suit and became counts. Although they seem to have recognized a formal obligation

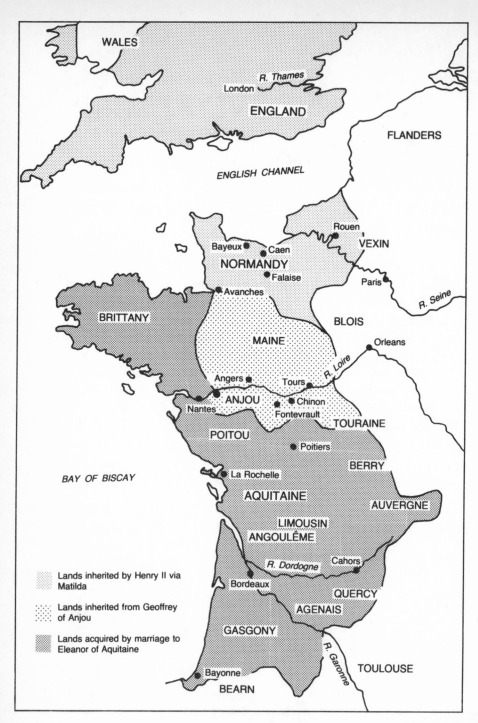

WALES

R. Thames

London

ENGLAND

FLANDERS

ENGLISH CHANNEL

Rouen

VEXIN

Bayeux Caen

NORMANDY

Falaise

Paris

Avanches

R. Seine

BRITTANY

BLOIS

MAINE

Orleans

R. Loire

Angers   Tours

Chinon

ANJOU

Nantes   Fontevrault

TOURAINE

POITOU

Poitiers

BERRY

La Rochelle

AQUITAINE

AUVERGNE

BAY OF BISCAY

LIMOUSIN

ANGOULÊME

R. Dordogne   Cahors

Lands inherited by Henry II via Matilda

Bordeaux

QUERCY

Lands inherited from Geoffrey of Anjou

AGENAIS

Lands acquired by marriage to Eleanor of Aquitaine

GASGONY

R. Garonne

TOULOUSE

Bayonne

BEARN

The Angevin empire in 1154.

to the kings of France, the self-declared counts of Anjou were effectively independent. They then set about turning a small county into a considerably larger one. There were only two really effective ways of doing this in the Middle Ages. One was to kill your neighbours and take their lands; the other was to marry their daughters in the hope that you or your children might inherit their lands. The Angevins proved remarkably adept at both methods.

The end result was that by the early eleventh century they had more than doubled the size of the lands they ruled. The county of Touraine had been conquered by 1044; Vendôme was acquired by marriage. They also campaigned with some success along their borders with Brittany and Poitou. North of Anjou, the counts set their sights on the county of Maine. Here they ran into competition from another neighbour — William the Conqueror, Duke of Normandy. This rivalry with Normandy continued into the reign of Henry I of England, but the final victory went to Anjou in 1110 when the French King Henry II's grandfather, Count Fulk V, married the daughter of the last Count of Maine.

Henry I was not pleased, but he already had too many enemies without fighting Anjou. Instead, he changed policies and proposed a marriage alliance. Henry's son William would marry Count Fulk's daughter. The wedding was celebrated in 1119, but only a year later the groom was drowned when crossing the Channel in the disaster of the White Ship.

For Henry this was not only a personal, but a political, disaster. Apart from a daughter, Matilda, married to the Emperor of Germany, Henry I had no other legitimate children. The best claimants to the succession were also Henry's bitterest foes. Robert, Henry's elder brother, had been a prisoner in England since 1104, when he lost the battle for Normandy. However, Robert's son, William Clito, was free and gaining new supporters every day.

It was not until after 1125, when Matilda's husband died, that Henry was able to recall her to England and proclaim her his heir. By this time William Clito had gained the support of the King of France and was putting together a coalition to solve Henry's succession problems by depriving him of all his lands. Henry I needed allies to support him in the coming struggle. He also needed to find a new husband for Matilda to defend her rights in the future. Once again, he approached Count Fulk V of Anjou. In 1128, Fulk's eldest son and heir, Geoffrey, was married to Matilda. Their first son, Henry, was born five years later.

Henry II was eventually to rule all the lands of both his Norman and

Angevin ancestors. But did anyone plan this, or did it simply happen? Those historians who tend to see the continental lands as an encumbrance, rather than an asset, tend to feel the whole thing was a dreadful mistake. Henry I, they argue, never intended to combine Anjou with the Anglo-Norman state, nor to have Count Geoffrey of Anjou rule in England. Count Geoffrey was simply to act as a hired soldier defending his wife's rights and the eventual succession of his son Henry. When Henry II reached maturity, he would take over England and Normandy, and Anjou would go its own separate way, eventually to be inherited by another son of Geoffrey.

Whether it was realistic to think that a husband could be excluded from his wife's property in this period is questionable. More importantly, the point has been made that Henry I's plans for events after his death did not really matter that much. The question was what Matilda's husband Geoffrey had in mind, and to a ruler of Anjou the prospect of ruling Normandy as well was almost certainly an attractive one. The proof is that Geoffrey spent the decade following Henry I's death making sure he did become ruler of Normandy.

William Clito, the main threat to Matilda's succession, died in 1128. Instead it was another nephew, Stephen of Blois, who seized the crown when Henry I died in 1135. While Matilda waged fruitless war up and down England, her husband Geoffrey set about the systematic conquest of Normandy, completed by 1144. From then on he ruled Normandy together with Anjou until 1150 when he made his young son, Henry, duke. In the following year he died, and Henry II succeeded him as Count of Anjou.

A curious story told by an English chronicler, William of Newburgh, writing sixty years later, relates that it was not Henry, but his younger brother Geoffrey, who was supposed to inherit Anjou. The story William tells is this. Count Geoffrey on his deathbed decided to leave Anjou to his younger son Geoffrey. Henry was to rule Anjou only until he had regained England from Stephen, when he was to give Anjou to his brother Geoffrey. The illness had been sudden, and Henry was absent, so the dying count made all those present promise not to bury his body until Henry had sworn to obey his father's last will. In due course, the count died, Henry arrived and was asked to swear the oath. The odd thing is that Henry II was apparently kept in ignorance of the contents of the will to which he was required to swear. This makes it a much better story, for we are left to imagine Henry II's rage when, having held out for days while his father's body mouldered in the chapel next door, he finally gave in with a flood of tears, only to find that he had sworn away Anjou. Medieval chroniclers were always fond of deathbed scenes, where death, the great leveller, humbled even the mightiest princes. A dash of the macabre, as provided by the count's decomposing body, was even better.

What the story does not tell us, however, is that a division of Anjou and Normandy was expected to follow Count Geoffrey's death. On the contrary, it shows the decision to split up the inheritance as a sudden deathbed change of plan by Geoffrey. The whole thrust of the story, the witnesses sworn to secrecy, the desperate measures to secure Henry's assent, serves to emphasize the fact that something unusual and rather surprising was being done here, and the story loses its point unless Henry himself expected to succeed to Anjou. Geoffrey had been ruling Normandy since 1144 and if, as the story suggests, he had not originally planned to leave Anjou to his son Geoffrey, then he must have been intending to give it to Henry. Even if we believe the story, it still shows that most of the time, most people must have expected Anjou and Normandy to be joined together at the old count's death.

In some ways the story itself is inherently improbable. In 1151, when Geoffrey died, Matilda's struggle against Stephen had come to a standstill. The question was whether Henry II could keep Normandy, not conquer England; and if he never conquered England, then he would never have to hand over Anjou. Unburied bodies had few spiritual rights at this time and the count was effectively risking his immortal soul for his younger son. Yet when we look at his legacy it turns out to have been more of a sweepstake ticket than a real inheritance.

Whatever the truth of the matter, Henry II did go on to become King of England while keeping both Normandy and Anjou. Before this, he had an unexpected addition to his fortunes. The marriage between Eleanor of Aquitaine and King Louis VII had lasted fifteen years and produced only two daughters. In this period, that was more than enough reason for a royal divorce and relations between the king and queen had been strained ever since they had quarrelled on the Second Crusade in 1148. No one was particularly surprised, therefore, when in March 1152, Louis VII quietly had his marriage annulled. What did surprise people was that only weeks later Eleanor married the new Count of Anjou and pretender to the English throne, Henry II.

Although Louis VII had divorced Eleanor he can have had little intention of giving up her lands. In fact, arrangements had already been made to marry off her daughters to allies of Louis VII who would eventually succeed to Eleanor's rights in Aquitaine. The proper thing for Eleanor to do in this situation would have been to retire to one of the more fashionable convents. But Eleanor was not the nunnery type, and in Henry II she found a man more than capable of defending her lands. Louis VII was furious and promptly attacked Henry II. He was joined by King Stephen's son Eustace and Henry's own brother Geoffrey who, whatever the truth of his father's will, really did want to be Count of Anjou.

Despite this opposition, Henry II was able not only to hold his own on the Continent, but to continue with his plans for the invasion of England, where he landed in January 1153. In November, after the unexpected death of his son and heir Eustace in August, Stephen came to terms with Henry II and named him as his heir. Before Stephen conveniently died, Henry II had time to return to the Continent and complete his victory over Louis VII. In August 1154, Louis VII recognized Henry II not only as Count of Anjou and Duke of Normandy, but also as Duke of Aquitaine. It was only a few months later that news of Stephen's death was carried over the Channel and Henry assumed the last of his titles — king. The Angevin empire, if such it was, had been born.

Explanations for Henry's phenomenal success in such a short space of time have abounded. Contemporaries saw the hand of God behind the king, while historians have preferred the workings of Providence. Both have been quick to acknowledge Henry's very real abilities as a soldier and politician. To understand Henry II's victory over Louis VII, however, one must also appreciate the geography of his lands. Louis VII had ruled Aquitaine for fifteen years. On the surface, for Henry II to be able to deprive him of it, while simultaneously preparing the conquest of England, sounds a tall order indeed. But the relative positions of a French king and a count of Anjou trying to control Aquitaine were very different. Louis VII's lands and resources were concentrated in a small area around Paris and Orléans. Although as king he could lay claim to a tradition of wider authority, and in practice exert considerable influence over bishoprics outside his immediate domains, he had no knights or castles to call on near the borders of Aquitaine. In fact, even to get there was tricky; the quickest way was straight through Anjou. Anjou, on the other hand, did have common borders with Aquitaine.

In fact, Aquitaine was just one of many areas into which the Angevins had been expanding throughout the past two centuries. The union of

Aquitaine and Capetian France was unworkable, as Louis's fifteen ineffectual years as duke had shown. The union of Anjou and Aquitaine was not only workable, but the culmination of two centuries of Angevin pressure. It also made certain that Henry would retain personal control of Anjou, for Anjou was the vital centre through which communications between Henry's northern and southern lands must pass.

Anjou in fact had common borders with all Henry's continental lands. It was not only the spiritual but also the geographical centre of the Angevin lands — Henry after all was born, died and buried there, and now lies alongside his wife Eleanor and son Richard in the Abbey of Fontevrault.

What did Angevin rule mean in practice for England and Henry's other lands? Unlike the Norman Conquest of 1066, it did not mean government being taken over by 'foreigners'. England and Normandy continued to be ruled by Normans, Poitou by Poitevins and Brittany by Bretons. Each state had its own administration and its own officers. This has often been compared unfavourably to England and Normandy under Henry I, where some historians have seen a tendency to draw the Church and administration of the two into a single 'Anglo-Norman Regnum'. But then Henry II's lands were not an empire in the sense that the British or Roman empires were. Henry ruled in each of his lands, as the legitimate ruler, according to the laws and customs of that land.

This is not to say that Angevin rule marked no change at all. In the first place, ruling several lands made Henry II very much more powerful in any one of them than he would have been otherwise. As a ruler Henry might claim only his rights, but it was Henry who defined those rights, and the resources of all his lands could be brought to bear on anyone foolish enough to disagree.

Secondly, Henry II and Richard were absent not only from England, but also from their other lands most of the time. This meant that another result of Angevin rule was the development of separate administrations which could handle the machinery of government in the king's absence. How effective this machinery of government was is shown by the way it was able to cope with Richard I's long absence on crusade and as a prisoner in Germany.

The fact that these lands were now ruled by one man meant that there was no longer any reason for them to go to war with each other. This was good news for people who lived in border regions that had seen regular devastation for centuries. It was also good news for anyone who wanted to travel across these borders and make a profit selling goods. Medieval trade was often a dangerous profession. In 1186, when Philip Augustus was having a disagreement with Henry II, he 'ordered that all those from the King of England's lands, found in the country should be seized along with their goods'. Henry retaliated by ordering the arrest of any French merchants. A few years later, Raymond of Toulouse tried to get at Richard I by arresting merchants from his lands: 'Some of whom he deprived of their eyes and testicles, some of whom he killed, and the rest of whom he imprisoned'.

Within the Angevin lands a merchant could reasonably hope not to lose any limbs to international politics. Henry's lands in fact included nearly all the major ports of north-western Europe: London, Bristol, Rouen, Nantes, La Rochelle, Bordeaux and Bayonne. The wine trade from Bordeaux to England continues to this day. The southern lands also produced salt, which was exchanged for cloth, tin and grain. Trade followed inland routes along the great river systems of the Seine, Loire and Garonne. The towns, which benefited most, showed their appreciation of the fact by consistently supporting the Angevin kings in times of rebellion and invasion.

All this was probably incidental to Henry's main purposes. Although as a ruler he acknowledged responsibilities to his subjects, the lands he held he ruled for the benefit of himself and his family. His different dominions were important to him because each of them added to his total wealth and power. As one contemporary said of Richard I, he was

> extremely rich in land and resources, much more so than the King of France. He could raise a very large army from his vassals and mercenaries, for he could summon English, Normans, Bretons, Manceaux, Angevins, and Poitevins.

The key to understanding the Angevin empire lies simply in that — the ability of one ruler to bring together troops and taxes from a variety of lands. In this way, Henry II was able to use the lands he had in 1154 to acquire during the course of his reign the whole of Brittany, disputed lands between Anjou and Champagne, the Norman Vexin on the border between France and Normandy, Cahors and Quercy bordering Toulouse and Aquitaine. Until the changes of Philip Augustus's reign, Henry II was constantly expanding, both in territory and in actual influence. In the 1170s, his attentions were concentrated in that area of central France which included Berry, Auvergne and the Limousin. For the most part, he was successful, just as in Britain he was able to impose himself on Ireland, Wales and Scotland. Until the birth of Philip Augustus in 1165, it looked as if France itself would go to the Angevins, for Louis VII's heir was his eldest daughter Margaret, engaged in 1158 to Henry's eldest son and name-sake.

The birth of a male heir to the kingdom of France made it almost inevitable that the struggles of Louis VII and Henry II would be resumed in the next generation. But most historians have seen Henry's biggest threat in 'the needless grasping, treacherous ambitions of his quarrelsome sons'.

Henry II was determined that all of his children should rule as princes. Richard, as the second son, was earmarked soon after birth for Aquitaine, the maternal inheritance. Geoffrey, the next in line, was taken care of in 1169, when it was arranged he should marry the heiress to Brittany and rule there as count. Henry, as the eldest, was to have the lion's share: England, Normandy and Anjou. Following the traditions of his Angevin forefathers, Henry wanted all his children acknowledged as rulers of their respective territories while he was still alive. In 1170, he had Henry crowned king in England. The following year, in a similar ceremony, Richard became Duke of Aquitaine. Geoffrey was already calling himself Count of Brittany. The problem was that, although Henry wanted his sons to be acknowledged as rulers, he still expected to go on running things as before. His sons however had different ideas.

In 1173, when the eldest was only nineteen, the three brothers Henry, Richard and Geoffrey joined their mother in a rebellion against Henry. It took Henry two years to bring his family to heel. Eleanor he imprisoned for the rest of his reign. With his sons, however, he was more generous. Indeed, he went some way to meeting their demands. Richard I was given enough power in Aquitaine to begin a relentless series of campaigns against the restless baronage. Henry and Geoffrey both received a portion of the revenues that went with their titles. Later, Geoffrey also began to assume some of his duties in Brittany. It was Henry, the eldest, who was forced to live most in his father's shadow and so remained discontented. Eventually, he again turned against his father in 1183, only to die of a sudden fever, sent by God it was rumoured, for his filial impiety and his plundering of monastic property to pay his troops.

Henry II's suggestion that Richard, as the new heir of Normandy, England and Anjou, should now pass on Aquitaine to John, the youngest of the brothers, resulted in intermittent family strife over the next six years. Henry's last words to Richard were rumoured to have been 'God grant that I may not die until I have had my just revenge on you.'

Colourful and unedifying though all this is, it should not distract our attention from the practical realities of Henry II's succession. The argument that 'these schemes for division will not allow any but the most elementary conception of an Angevin Empire' is not as straightforward as it might appear. It was always planned that the eldest of Henry's children, first Henry and then Richard, should rule in Normandy, England and Anjou. In other words, all the lands that Henry II had inherited from his parents were now regarded as indivisible. It was only the lands that he himself had acquired, by marriage, diplomacy or conquest, with which he was prepared to endow his other children.

Secondly, those lands that were to go to younger sons remained answerable to the head of the family. The younger Henry did homage to Louis VII in 1169 for Brittany, and it was only then that Geoffrey began calling himself count. Similarly, Henry II's insistence that Richard do homage to his elder brother for Aquitaine was an important element in the complex family quarrel that erupted in 1183. Richard's refusal to give up Aquitaine to John later was not an attempt to 'grab the lot' and reunite lands Henry II wanted to divide. It was simply a question of a bird in the hand being worth Normandy, England and Anjou in the bush. In the same way, Richard refused in 1188 to let Henry II bargain away lands Richard had conquered in Toulouse, to save lands captured by Philip Augustus, 'which he did not rule, but were only promised to him'. Once Richard was actually ruling the other lands, he was quite happy to put someone else in charge of Aquitaine, although he chose his German nephew Otto rather than John. The new lordship of Ireland, which was all Henry II could find to give John in the end, was still subject to the King of England. When John rebelled in Richard's reign, Richard promptly confiscated Ireland.

When Richard I died, struck by an arrow under the walls of Chalus, he left two possible heirs: John, and Geoffrey of Brittany's son Arthur. Who had the better right to succeed: a younger brother or a nephew in the senior line? England and Normandy decided on the former, while Anjou chose Arthur. What is revealing is that, despite different local customs, neither candidate seems to have considered splitting up the empire. John's victory made him the third king of England in a row to rule Normandy, Anjou and Aquitaine, as well as claiming rights over

Brittany, Toulouse and Flanders. He was also the last, but that was because he lost the long fight against Philip Augustus. Had John won instead of lost, it seems more than likely that the Angevin empire would have been passed on intact to his son, and the shape of European history would look very different indeed.

CHAPTER VII

GERMANY AND ENGLAND 1066–1453

Benjamin Arnold

IN ALMOST EVERY REIGN from the Norman Conquest of 1066 to the fall of Bordeaux in 1453 and even later, the rulers of England took the view that their kingdom provided a rich foundation for wider political and diplomatic schemes in which their power and their glory would make a mark upon continental Europe as well. This is not surprising, considering that the kings of England were themselves dukes of Normandy and counts of Anjou until 1204, and dukes of Aquitaine until 1453. From 1337 Edward III and his successors hoped to restore their influence on the Continent by their daring claim to the crown of France itself. In similar style his son John of Gaunt, Duke of Lancaster, unsuccessfully laid claim to the kingdom of Castile between 1371 and 1389.

Such claims backed by armed force were by no means the only examples of English ambitions of this type. In agreement with the papacy, Henry III put forward his son Edmund of Lancaster as candidate for the throne of Sicily in 1254, a plan which foundered for lack of political, military and financial support from the English barons. In the event, it was Charles of Anjou, brother of King Louis IX of France, who wrested the Sicilian kingdom from the Staufen dynasty, a result ardently desired by the papacy. In 1257, however, Henry III's brother, Earl Richard of Cornwall, did succeed in having himself elected King of the Romans, the official title for the bearer of the German crown before his imperial coronation in Rome by a party of German princes headed by Archbishop Conrad of Cologne. Largely for commercial reasons, the archdiocese of Cologne had always favoured an alliance with England. However, the powers of the German crown had been rendered so ineffective by civil conflict since 1240 that King Richard achieved nothing during his several visits from England to the Rhineland, the only part of Germany where he enjoyed any support. According to a German annalist, the king poured out money like water at the feet of the princes in order to raise his prestige, and no doubt the renowned wealth of the English royal house was what had attracted the electors to Richard of Cornwall in the first place.

Since Richard was the candidate of only one party in Germany, he was never able to establish himself successfully against the claim of his rival, Alfonso X of Castile, also elected in 1257. But at least Richard visited Germany, which Alfonso never did, and in 1267 he married as his third wife a German noblewoman, Beatrice of Valkenburg. King Richard died in 1272. Despite his lack of success as a German king, this was not the only time that a Plantagenet was considered for the throne of the German Empire. In 1348, part of the German electoral college of princes elected Edward III as King of the Romans in opposition to the pro-French king elected in 1346, Charles of Bohemia, later the Emperor Charles IV. But Edward's brother-in-law, Margrave William of Jülich, persuaded him that there was no real future to his candidacy, so the king decided to renounce his claim and to recognize Charles IV for the sake of peace. During the 1390s, when the German electors were preparing to depose Charles IV's incompetent son Wenceslas IV, they considered electing Richard II of England in his place. Eventually, they decided upon one of their own number, the Elector Rupert of the Rhine. But, when Rupert died in 1410, Henry IV of England's name was one of those put forward in the electoral college for consideration.

These pro-English electoral manoeuvres, and the reign of Richard of Cornwall itself, testify to the diplomatic alignment of Germany and England in the Middle Ages which can first be discerned in Otto the Great's marriage to Eadgyth of Wessex in 929. We know that there were profitable trading connections between England, the Rhineland and northern Germany in the eleventh century, and that German merchants, 'men of the emperor', were to be seen in London. The rise of Anglo-Norman power under William the Conqueror and Henry I of England appears to have motivated the German imperial court under the Salian dynasty to seek a direct alliance with the Norman house, possibly because both parties shared an interest in outfacing the claims and decrees of the reformed papacy against the exercise of unfettered royal authority over the Church in England and Germany. Another motive can be discerned in the adventurous marriage policy of the Salian house, which had previously sought brides from Denmark, France, Lombardy and Russia. For various reasons, these countries had rather fallen in estimation in Germany, and the Salian ruler Henry V apparently hoped to find a reliable ally in Henry I of England.

For this purpose Henry I's daughter Matilda, twin sister of the Anglo-Norman heir William, was betrothed to Henry V in 1110, and a dowry of 10,000 silver marks was dispatched to the impecunious groom. Amid scenes of splendour the marriage took place at Mainz in 1114, attended by five German archbishops, thirty bishops, five dukes and a host of counts and abbots. In 1117 Matilda was crowned empress in Rome, Henry V's own imperial coronation having taken place in 1111. When her brother was drowned in 1120, the empress became the prospective heiress of Normandy and England. Had Matilda's first marriage proved fruitful, then it is likely that Germany and England would have been united under the Salian house just as Sicily and Germany were united by means of an analogous marriage under the Staufen imperial house in 1194.

When Henry V died in 1125, Henry I insisted that the childless empress should return to his court. He arranged for her to marry Count Geoffrey of Anjou with a view to their future as rulers of Normandy and England. However, Matilda's rights in England were cast aside when Stephen of Blois seized the throne in 1135 and it was only after years of civil conflict that the claims of Henry II, son of Geoffrey and Matilda, were recognized. He succeeded Stephen as King of England in 1154, keen to revive his grandfather Henry I's alliance with the German Empire as the leading European power of the time. Although Henry I had been on bad terms with the French court, the original alliance of 1110 was not motivated by any German hostility for France. In the Middle Ages, France and Germany did not have good reason for viewing each other as enemies. Armed conflicts were few and far between, although some of the German territorial princes were often tempted by English money to play a part in the Hundred Years War against the French. In 1124, however, Emperor Henry V did decide to offer his father-in-law military support against Louis VI of France. As Henry I advanced upon Paris from Normandy, Henry V created a diversion in eastern France. According to Abbot Suger of St Denis, these incursions were turned back by divine intervention.

The marriage of Henry V and Matilda of Normandy inaugurated a tradition, punctuated by disputes, in which the German and English courts were aligned, a tradition which outlasted the Middle Ages. This *entente cordiale* again began to have practical consequences in the 1160s when Henry II of England and Emperor Frederick I Barbarossa shared a compelling interest in overthrowing the pretensions of the papacy under Pope Alexander III (1159–81). His very title to the papacy had been rejected by the emperor at the Council of Pavia in 1160, a meeting to which Henry II had sent ambassadors. In 1164 Henry II proclaimed the Constitutions of Clarendon, in effect a defiance of the papacy, and in 1165 the emperor's principal adviser, Archbishop Rainald of Cologne, arrived in Rouen to formalize the revived alliance between England and Germany. At the same time, an English embassy to the imperial court conveyed Henry II's recognition of Frederick Barbarossa's antipope, Pachal III. At the end of the year the emperor visited Charlemagne's tomb at Aachen and caused the greatest of his imperial predecessors to be canonized, thus underlining the spiritual quality of the authority that Barbarossa, as an emperor, claimed over the entire western Church. For the purpose of this canonization, the emperor almost certainly borrowed Henry II's papal certificate for the canonization of Edward the Confessor at Westminster in 1161 and announced that Charlemagne's elevation to sainthood had taken place at the English king's request.

Henry II and the German emperor had already been in touch during the 1150s, resulting in one of the more extraordinary diplomatic exchanges of the Middle Ages. The background is as follows. When Empress Matilda left Germany in 1125, she took with her several trophies, including an important relic from the imperial treasury, the hand of St James. Upon such prestigious relics, including the supposed Holy Lance, a fragment of the True Cross and soil soaked in the blood of the protomartyr Stephen, the welfare and stability of the German Empire were considered, in part, to rest. So Frederick Barbarossa sent a message to Henry II to request the return of the hand of St James. Matilda had meanwhile deposited it at her father's magnificent foundation and mausoleum at Reading and Henry II had no intention of depriving the abbey of an asset much more significant than his grandfather's tomb.

In 1157, the King of England sent ambassadors to Frederick Barbarossa 'to bestow varied and precious gifts, enhanced by much graceful language', as the emperor's biographers noted, but the hand of St James remained at Reading Abbey. The embassy also brought an extremely effusive letter from Henry II which, in line with the diplomatic usage and political theory of the time, implicitly recognized that the emperor was the lord of the whole Christian world. As translated by C. C. Mierow and R. Emery, it included the following passage:

> We lay before you our kingdom and whatever is anywhere subject to our
> sway [i.e. Henry II's lands in France], and entrust it to your power, that
> all things may be administered in accordance with your nod, and that in
> all respects your imperial will may be done. Let there be, therefore,
> between us and our peoples an undivided unity of affection and peace, safe
> commercial intercourse, yet so that to you, who excel us in worth, may
> fall the right to command; while we shall not lack the will to obey.

Obviously it was not Henry II's real intention to submit his English
kingdom and his French lands to German sovereignty, but he did
mean to assure Frederick Barbarossa that an emperor was, in a sense
which transcended actual political arrangements, the real suzerain of
Christendom.

Not all Englishmen approved of the German emperors' pretension to
this type of world dominion. As W. J. Miller et al. point out, at the time
of the Council of Pavia, when Frederick Barbarossa in effect tried to
impose his own preference as pope, Victor IV, upon the whole Church,
John of Salisbury recorded in anger:

> Who has appointed the Germans to be judges of the nations? Who has
> given authority to brutal and headstrong men that they should set up a
> prince of their own choosing over the heads of the sons of men? In truth
> their madness has often attempted to do this, but by God's will, it has on
> each occasion been overthrown and put to confusion, and they have
> blushed for their own iniquity.

In the manner of diplomacy between royal dynasties, the pact sealed at
Rouen in 1165 stipulated two betrothals. Henry II's infant daughter
Eleanor was betrothed to the emperor's small son and heir Frederick. But
the latter did not survive childhood and eventually Eleanor married the
King of Castile. The second betrothal was between the emperor's cousin
and close ally, Henry the Lion, Duke of Saxony and Bavaria, and Henry
II's eldest daughter Matilda. This marriage did take place, at Minden in
Saxony in 1168, and from it descended the Welf house of Brunswick
which eventually succeeded to the British throne in 1714. Henry the Lion
was the most powerful, but at the same time the most arrogant, prince
in Germany and, although the emperor never regarded him as a threat, a
consortium of north German bishops and nobles insisted in 1179 that the
duke be deposed as a public menace. To this Frederick Barbarossa
reluctantly agreed and, after a series of legal procedures and military

campaigns, Saxony and Bavaria were confiscated. Henry the Lion, Matilda and their children travelled as exiles to Henry II's court. The King of England did not permit the duke's fall to upset his alliance with the German Empire. Nevertheless, the Angevin and Staufen houses did fall out in the 1190s, that is, after the deaths of Henry II (1189) and Frederick Barbarossa (1190). The reasons for this are to be found in the history of the Third Crusade.

The sources relate that Richard I of England and Duke Leopold V of Austria quarrelled about their respective rights in Acre after it had fallen to the crusaders, the enraged king throwing down the duke's banner from the walls with his own hands. Richard I may have got the better of this argument, but the duke had his revenge when the king rashly decided to return to England by crossing the German Empire in disguise. Recognized in Austrian territory, he was arrested and imprisoned by the duke. When news of this reached Frederick Barbarossa's son and successor, Emperor Henry VI, he decided to use the opportunity to turn England from an ally into a dependency of the German Empire. He purchased the prisoner from Duke Leopold V, incarcerated him at Trifels Castle in the Rhineland and demanded that a huge ransom be levied in England. He also extracted an oath of homage from Richard I, thus converting England into a vassal kingdom under the Empire. In 1194, when Richard had agreed to these terms, he was released. A German chronicler claimed that the ransom arrived upon a train of fifty pack-horses, which is a possibility if the 150,000 silver marks were packed in barrels. Although England and Germany were still aligned, it was upon very much worse terms for England than those agreed at Rouen in 1165. However, Richard I seems to have borne very little resentment of his treatment.

When Emperor Henry VI died suddenly in 1197, Germany and England became involved in a new and unexpected way. In 1196 Henry VI had secured the succession of his infant son Frederick II, but now Archbishop Adolf of Cologne, envious of the Archbishop of Mainz's rights as the premier elector to the German crown, decided to stage a counter-election of his own. The problem was to find a suitable candidate, let alone a credible electoral college. Duke Berthold V of Zähringen having prudently declined the proffered crown, the Archbishop of Cologne alighted upon Otto of Brunswick, the second surviving son of Henry the Lion and Matilda of Anjou. Otto accepted the offer and was elected by a small minority of princes in 1198. As a nephew of Richard I, Otto had been appointed Count of Poitou in 1196 and now the King of England decided to extend him money and political support for the German adventure, largely because his elevation to the throne at the hands of a party centred upon Cologne again underlined the community of commercial interest between that city and London. His nephew's election also released Richard I from any threat of a renewal of his status as a vassal of the Empire.

The Welfs of Brunswick were proud of their imperial descent. When their grand new church of St Blaise in Brunswick was dedicated in 1188, a memorial inscription recorded Duchess Matilda as 'daughter of King Henry II of England, son of Matilda, Empress of the Romans' and Henry the Lion as 'son of the daughter of the Emperor Lothair', who had reigned from 1125 until 1137. But it is a mistake to suppose that the Welfs nursed a desire, based upon exalted lineage, to wrest the German Empire from the Staufen dynasty in revenge for Henry the Lion's deposition in 1180, as certain thirteenth-century sources seem to imply. The choice of Otto of Brunswick and Poitou in 1198 was fortuitous, the result of Berthold of Zähringen's refusal.

Since the infant King Frederick II was absent in Sicily at his mother's court, the Staufen party in Germany reacted to the crisis by electing Henry VI's formidable brother, Duke Philip of Swabia, as their king. Although Otto IV had secured the backing of the papacy for his election — in 1199 he wrote to Pope Innocent III that 'after the death of our uncle King Richard, you are our only comfort and succour' — it was not until King Philip's assassination in a private quarrel in 1208 that the Welf king's title was secure in Germany. By this date Otto IV's other uncle, King John of England who had succeeded Richard I in 1199, was interested in setting up a new alliance against France in order to assist him to recover Anjou and Normandy, his possessions confiscated by King Philip II in 1204.

Otto IV played for time. He was much more interested in establishing his authority in the Italian peninsula, the second kingdom in the Empire after Germany, than in adventures in France. But his plans went wrong. He overplayed his hand in Italy in attempting to subject the papacy to his own temporal control, a state of affairs to which Innocent III could never submit. At about the same time, therefore, as King John was finding himself at odds with the pope over his high-handed treatment of the English Church and baronage, Otto IV also fell from favour at the papal *Curia*. So the two disgraced rulers decided to avenge themselves upon Innocent III's principal ally, Philip II of France, and embarked upon the campaigns which ended in a complete French victory at the Battle of Bouvines in 1214. King John had to accept the loss of his northern French possessions and Otto IV fled back to Saxony.

This disaster marked the end of the Welf-Angevin alliance. King John was constrained to submit to the demands of the papacy, the English Church and the barons. He died in 1216. Otto IV surrendered the Empire to Frederick II, who had arrived in arms from Sicily in 1212 to claim his German inheritance. Otto retired to his own castles and died in 1218. Frederick II was a traditionalist and an astute diplomat; he sought to establish a lasting trust between England, Germany, the papacy and France, a situation which had only rarely been achieved in the twelfth century. Since everyone was oppressed by memories of the violent confrontations of the period from 1198 to 1214, there was hope for *détente*. But the policy was only partially successful, due to the papacy's fear of the resurgence of imperial power, especially in Italy, under Frederick II's capable government. However, one fruit of this phase matured in 1235, with Frederick II's marriage to Isabella of England, sister of Henry III. She was the emperor's fourth wife and bore him four children before her death in childbirth in 1241.

The marriage of 1235, which was in its motivation reminiscent of the marriage of Isabella's great-grandmother Matilda to Henry V in 1114, did not result in a lasting alliance between England and Germany. For reasons of papal policy, Gregory IX excommunicated Frederick II in 1239 and, as a loyal member of the Church, Henry III correctly but uncharitably broke off relations with the imperial court. As mentioned above, the election of his brother Richard of Cornwall as King of the Romans in 1257 was a pro-papal candidacy intended to exclude Frederick II's descendants from any part in German kingship.

In spite of Richard of Cornwall's ineffectiveness as a German king, the episode did at least restore the tradition that England and Germany ought to be aligned. For this reason Edward I of England arranged with his contemporary, Rudolf I of Habsburg, King of the Romans, a betrothal of their children Joan of Acre and Hartmann of Habsburg. However, Hartmann died in an accident before the marriage itself could take place. In the fourteenth century the relation of the two courts tended to be influenced by the rhythm of English interest in France. In 1337, for example, when Edward III claimed the crown of France, he drew his brother-in-law, Emperor Louis IV the Bavarian, into an alliance against

France. The emperor hoped to use this treaty as a means to threaten the papacy, which at that period resided at Avignon on the confines of the French kingdom. The *Curia* at Avignon was his principal enemy and, since it was in general a pro-French power, the alliance with England appeared logical. Although nothing tangible resulted from his English treaty, the earnestness of the emperor's hopes can be measured from the fact that Edward III was appointed Vicar of the Empire, that is, the emperor's representative with sovereign powers to act as he saw fit during such time as he was upon imperial soil. The English king's right to this title lasted from 1338 to 1341, when the alliance with Louis the Bavarian collapsed. According to H. S. Offler, Edward III's vicariate was intended to give him the necessary authority as overlord for holding together the military alliance of princes in the Rhineland and the Netherlands which had been set up, with English subsidies, to oppose the French. In spite of the contretemps of 1341, the marriage in 1382 of Richard II of England to Anne of Bohemia, the sister of Wenceslas IV, King of the Romans, was intended to demonstrate the continued tenacity of the diplomatic tradition of amity stretching back to the early twelfth century.

So far, the focus has been on relations between England and Germany at the level of diplomacy and high politics — on the comings and goings of envoys and on the misunderstandings that followed upon the activities of the two courts. But England and Germany were also aligned in a much wider sphere through the commercial interests that bound the two countries. London was, after all, one of the four major terminal depots, with Novgorod in Russia, Bruges in Flanders and Bergen in Norway, of the most effective mercantile organization in northern Europe, the German Hansa, which reached the height of its prosperity in the thirteenth and fourteenth centuries. German commercial shipping dominated the North and Baltic seas, and so beneficial was the trade which the Germans exercised between England and the Continent that the English crown was glad to recognize the rights of the merchants of Cologne, Lübeck, Hamburg and other Hansa cities in the ports of England, especially London.

In his letter of 1157 to Frederick Barbarossa, Henry II had already mentioned the desirability of *commertia tuta*, secure commerce. Although the phrase itself is lifted from the classics, in the same year Henry II issued a privilege for the merchants of Cologne, offering them protection for their warehouse in London, the Guildhall, and permitting them to sell German wine on the same favourable terms as the sale of French wine. Later, the Hansa merchants in London moved their factory to the *Stalhof*, Steelyard, for the storage and sale of their merchandise, although the legal details of its constitution are not well known before the fifteenth century. However, we do know that by the end of the thirteenth century two aldermen of the London depot to some extent integrated the Hansa merchants with the government of the City of London, and that, as Philippe Dollinger put it, 'the merchants of the Steelyard were responsible for manning and maintaining Bishopsgate, one of the entrances to the city.'

Commerce, crusading and the rise of the papacy were international phenomena which had a great influence upon the relations of England and Germany after 1100, but the enterprises to which they gave rise did not always endear the peoples of western Christendom to each other. German chroniclers thought that the English behaved perfidiously on the Third Crusade and, for the other side, John of Salisbury always considered the Germans to be untrustworthy and barbarous, especially in matters relating to the rights of the Holy See. An educated Englishman who knew better how to bridge the gap was Gervase of Tilbury. A student at the law school of Bologna, he saw service at the Angevin and Sicilian courts before joining the entourage of Otto IV. Although the information about his functions at the German court is sparse, he was one of Otto IV's secretaries and was rewarded with the title of Marshal of the Kingdom of Arles, the Burgundian realm which also belonged to the western Empire. His career survived the fall of Otto IV, and it is now thought that Gervase's last appointment (1223–34) was as provost of the Benedictine house of Ebstorf in Saxony.

Towards the end of Otto IV's reign, Gervase presented the emperor with a handbook he had compiled about the nature, geography and curiosities of the world, a work later entitled *Otia imperialia*, roughly translatable as 'Leisure Time for Emperors'. If the work was ever read out to Otto IV, he would not have been impressed with its opening harangue about the relation of priestly as against royal power, argued in favour of the former, the issue over which the German ruler had just been badly mauled by Pope Innocent III.

The writings of John of Salisbury and Gervase of Tilbury serve to show that medieval England and Germany did not share any deep understanding of each other's traditions and institutions. The same could be said of Bishop Otto of Freising, the greatest chronicler of the German twelfth century. Writing his global *History of the Two Cities* in the 1140s, the bishop claimed that in 1124 Henry I of England had advised his son-in-law to inflict a tax upon the German kingdom similar to that levied by the Anglo-Norman rulers in England. Bishop Otto records that the emperor was actually engaged upon this task when he died unexpectedly in 1125. This seems an unlikely tale. Even if Henry V had contemplated raising a general tax, there would be evidence of a mode of assent, a method of assessment and a machinery of collection, all of which are lacking. However, Otto of Freising was Henry V's nephew, and he may well have heard that when the emperor had complained of shortage of funds, his father-in-law, Henry I of England, had helpfully suggested taxation. But a German ruler would have known that it was not possible to raise taxes, except upon his own manors, forests and towns. So the suggestion that Henry V was parading in arms through the lower Rhineland in 1125 in order to raise a general tax seems improbable, especially as this suggestion was withdrawn from the relevant section of the bishop's later work, *The Deeds of Frederick I*.

Another misunderstanding about institutional traditions and possibilities occurred in a letter of 1257 from King Richard of Cornwall to his nephew in England, the Lord Edward. Since the king was the candidate of only one party in Germany, his arrival in the Rhineland not surprisingly precipitated a civil conflict in which his episcopal backers were involved:

> Look what spirited and warlike archbishops and bishops we have in Germany; I would count it not at all unprofitable to you if such were created in England, by whose function you would be secured against the importunate assault of rebellion.

The king forgets that German bishops with their large armed retinues had frequently challenged royal authority in Germany, and in any case the political traditions of the two countries were quite out of step in this respect. England's bishops were reformers, lawyers and men of letters, not princes with territorial jurisdictions like the German episcopate; they would have found the necessary armed retinues an incomprehensible, expensive nuisance, with little place in the social structure of their dioceses.

Although it was not difficult to travel between London and Cologne in the Middle Ages, Germany and England remained quite remote from each other in cultural and political, if not in commercial terms. Medieval England was more in tune with the culture of France and Italy, and the magnificent twelfth-century churches of Cologne, for example, did not influence English building techniques. But in politics the ruling élite in England did tend to perceive the French court, if not France as such, as the enemy. In spite of the Treaty of Paris in 1259, by which Louis IX and Henry III sought to reverse this attitude, it took even greater hold in the fourteenth and fifteenth centuries, the era of the Hundred Years War. On the other hand the Germans were generally perceived as a nation amicable to the English, whose remote ancestry as a people who had originally emigrated from Saxony was never forgotten in the Middle Ages.

CHAPTER VIII

THE FALL OF THE ANGEVIN EMPIRE

John Gillingham

O N 30 JULY 1202, KING JOHN was at Le Mans when a messenger arrived bearing desperate news. His mother, Eleanor of Aquitaine, the grand old lady of twelfth-century politics, had been trapped at Mirebeau and was on the point of falling into the hands of his enemies, headed by his nephew, Arthur of Brittany. Between Le Mans and Mirebeau in Poitou lay nearly 100 miles of twelfth-century roads. Forty-eight hours later, at dawn on 1 August, Arthur and his followers, having forced their way into the castle and driven Eleanor back into the keep, the last refuge, were enjoying a relaxed breakfast — pigeons were on the menu that day — secure in the belief that John was still far away, when their quiet meal was rudely interrupted by the sudden arrival of Eleanor's royal son. They went for their weapons and did their best to put up some show of resistance. But it was too late. The cat was already among the pigeons. By thinking and acting faster than they had imagined possible, John had turned the tables on his enemies. Now it was they who were in the trap and not one of them escaped. More than 200 knights were captured, half a dozen barons and, best of all, Arthur himself. John Lackland, once the runt of the Plantagenet litter, had defeated his enemies more decisively than ever his father or even his warrior brother, Richard the Lionheart, had been able to do. It was a magnificent victory. 'God be praised for our happy success,' he wrote in exultation.

Yet within two years of the triumph at Mirebeau, the Plantagenet dynasty had suffered blows from which it was never to recover. In April 1203 John's most powerful opponent, King Philip Augustus of France, sailed down the Loire and held court in the great hall built by Henry II at Saumur. In May 1204 the Capetian king's troops swept through Normandy, taking Argentan, Falaise, Caen, Bayeux and Lisieux in a mere three weeks. On 24 June 1204, the ducal city of Rouen surrendered. Then Philip turned south again and two months later, in August 1204, he entered Poitiers. Further south still, the army of Alfonso VIII, King of Castile, was overrunning Gascony. In the space of just two summers John's continental empire had collapsed like a house of cards. And in 1205 it looked as though worse was to follow as Philip Augustus laid plans to invade England and John took panic measures to defend the south and east coasts.

As it happened it was to be another eleven years before John had to face the grim reality of a Capetian army in England — for more than twelve months during 1216 and 1217 London itself was to be controlled by Philip's son Louis — and in the intervening years he managed to stem the tide and even recover some territories, in particular Gascony. But some of the losses suffered in 1203–4 had proved to be irreversible. Thus in the long history of English kingship these years mark an important turning-point. Since 1066 England had been ruled by Frenchmen; first by Normans and then by the Plantagenets of Anjou. It is not surprising to find that some modern English historians have, in effect, breathed a sigh of patriotic relief when discussing the loss of Anjou and Normandy. Now at last the Plantagenets were free to become true English rulers. They could shake off the incubus of the Continent, stay 'at home' and look after their 'real' subjects.

But this is not how it was. In reality John, as the French-speaking ruler of that vast assemblage of lands which historians are accustomed to call the Angevin empire, had been as much at home at Chinon, Rouen and Poitiers as at Westminster and Winchester. England gave him a royal crown and this meant that 'King of England' was always the first element in his title, but he was also 'Lord of Ireland, Duke of Normandy and Aquitaine, Count of Anjou'. The loss of Anjou and Normandy did not mean that an English king had lost two outlying provinces. It meant that the Plantagenet dynasty had lost both its homeland (Anjou) and its first great acquisition (Normandy). The heart of the Angevin empire had been torn out. This was a dynastic disaster of the first magnitude. How had it come to this? How had the victor of Mirebeau, the ruler of so many territories, succumbed so swiftly to Philip's assaults? The question is all the more puzzling because a glance at the map would seem to suggest, on the face of it, that the Angevins were far richer than their Capetian overlords.

One possible answer to the question might lie in the fact that the Capetians were indeed the overlords. As King of England John was sovereign but on the Continent he was the King of France's vassal and subject to his court. There is no doubt that legally speaking the King of France always held the upper hand. But was this necessarily decisive? In 1152–3 Louis VII of France, angered by Henry II's marriage to Eleanor of Aquitaine — whom Louis had just divorced — decided to take possession of all Henry's continental dominions. John's father, however, successfully defended his territories against Louis VII's attack. In 1202–4 John found himself, legally speaking, in the same position — but he failed to resist. What was decisive, in other words, was not Capetian suzerainty but something else, perhaps the personal qualities of the kings involved, perhaps the relative strengths of their kingdoms.

Thus another possible answer to the question might be that the strength of the Angevin empire was more apparent than real. It has indeed been suggested that by 1200 Philip Augustus was a wealthier king than John. If that were so then John's defeat was no disgrace. However the fragmentary state of the records — on both sides — means that it is not possible to calculate precisely the financial resources of either of them. The result, happily and unsurprisingly, is controversy — a debate between those who believe that John was simply outgunned by a more powerful opponent and those, like myself, who believe that John threw away a winning hand. In my view there is not much doubt that the overall resources of the Angevin empire were a good deal greater than those at the disposal of Philip Augustus. But it may well be the case that Philip was able to concentrate his resources in the critical theatre of war more effectively than John. In other words it is not just a question of resources, but also of the way those resources were used.

John's problem was that he was unable to mobilize the huge resources of his empire and bring them to bear in the armed struggle against Philip. Why was this? Was it John's fault? Or was it because the Angevin empire was a cumbersome political structure, administratively incoherent and over-extended when compared with the more compact Capetian kingdom? The difficulty with any explanation which puts the emphasis on the supposed structural weakness of the Angevin empire is the fact that in the years immediately preceding John's accession (i.e. 1194–8) it had been the Plantagenet ruler — Richard the Lionheart — who had held the upper hand in the war against the Capetians. The most obvious explanation of the fact that a winning war turned into a losing one is the change of commander. Other explanations won't do. It cannot, for example, be argued that John inherited a kingdom exhausted by his predecessor's reckless improvidence because the financial records of John's reign demonstrate that the English taxpayer was still capable of digging deep into his pocket. Indeed the capacity of John's government to raise revenue on a considerable scale is often cited approvingly by those impressed by his record as king. Moreover historians have sometimes forgotten that the costs of war had to be borne by both sides. There is no evidence to show either that Richard had been, in financial terms, a more oppressive king than Philip, or that, by 1199, his dominions were any more 'exhausted' than the Capetian kingdom.

When it comes down to it, John failed where Richard succeeded because he lacked his brother's political, diplomatic and military skills. He won the day at Mirebeau because he took his enemies by surprise — and he took them by surprise precisely because by 1202 they had grown accustomed to his inability to act decisively or give inspiring leadership. If Mirebeau had signalled the birth of a new and dynamic John, then the end of the story would have been very different. Unfortunately for John, however, he at once reverted to type. He was almost never to be found where the action was. When the main threat was to Anjou, as it was during the autumn and winter of 1202–3, then John was to be found in Normandy. When the main threat was in the Seine valley and the east of Normandy, as it was in the spring of 1203, then John was to be found in the west. When Philip launched his final great attack on Normandy in 1204, John was in England. For John, being lord of so many territories meant there was always somewhere else to run to.

There is more yet that can be learnt from the story of the action at Mirebeau. Who were John's enemies that day? And why were they in armed opposition to him? At their head, of course, was his nephew, Arthur of Brittany. No one could seriously hold John responsible for the hostility between him and his nephew. In trying to rule the whole Angevin empire, John was trying to hold together lands which did not yet automatically belong together. The empire was a recent creation. It had been cobbled together in a series of succession disputes, and it was quite on the cards that another succession dispute would pull it apart again. Given the norms of dynastic politics, the quarrel between John and Arthur that followed Richard's death in April 1199 was almost certainly unavoidable. It was only natural that Arthur would accept, and John reject, the decision of the barons of Anjou to acknowledge the son of an elder brother (i.e. Arthur, son of Geoffrey) rather than a younger brother (John). In the subsequent struggle for Anjou, John owed much to the active military support of the leading barons of Poitou, conspicuous among them Hugh of Lusignan and his kindred. With their help he quickly won the upper hand and, by January 1200, the Treaty of Le Goulet confirmed his position as the undisputed master of the whole Angevin empire.

But then, only seven months later, John made what most contemporary chroniclers regarded as the decisive mistake. He divorced his first wife and married Isabella, the twelve-year-old heiress to the country of Angoulême. In view of Angoulême's wealth and strategic importance — astride the vital lines of communcation between Poitiers and Bordeaux — there was much to be said in favour of this marriage. The problem was that Isabella was already betrothed — and to none other than Hugh of Lusignan. The Lusignans were understandably angry at being thus deprived of the prospect of succeeding to Angoulême. Perhaps, suitably compensated, they might have become reconciled to the loss, but John seems to have made little or no effort to placate them. In 1201 they rose in revolt and appealed for justice to Philip Augustus. Philip then pronounced the confiscation of all John's fiefs and awarded Poitou and Anjou to Arthur (April 1202). Thus the Lusignan revolt led directly to the reopening of the war of Angevin succession. Although Arthur was the nominal commander of the army which laid siege to Eleanor at Mirebeau, it was the Lusignans who provided the real driving force. The events at Mirebeau, in other words, reveal John's ability to make old enemies sink their differences and unite against him.

But as long as they were defeated — as John so stunningly defeated them at Mirebeau at breakfast time on 1 August 1202 — what did that matter? If the union of all those whose loyalty was suspect meant only that they could all be dealt with by a single crushing blow, then it might even be to the king's advantage if they were encouraged to unite. John won at Mirebeau, and that surely was all that mattered. Not quite. John, after all, had not won on his own. His coup at Mirebeau had only been possible with other men's help and advice. Prominent among the men who guided John to Mirebeau and who, on 1 August, fought their way into the town with him were two powerful barons: Aimeri of Thouars and William des Roches. Yet only a few weeks later, in September 1202, they were in rebellion against John. Indeed their capture of Angers, the chief city of Anjou, in October 1202, marked the beginning of the end of the Angevin empire. This surely is one of the most remarkable political about-turns of all time. The switch of Lusignan allegiance between 1199 and 1201 was rapid enough, one might have thought, but it was laboriously slow when compared with the shattering speed of this reversal. What on earth did Aimeri of Thouars and William des Roches think they were doing?

First, it has to be said that it was only with reluctance that the two of them had entered John's camp. But with the Lusignans against him, John badly needed support in this part of the world and their friendship was therefore well worth cultivating. In return for their help at Mirebeau they felt they were entitled to a voice in the king's counsel, in particular to a say in deciding what was to be done with the prisoners taken at Mirebeau. John, however, would not share the rewards of victory with anyone and, as a result, he lost the precarious friendship of these two magnates almost as soon as he had obtained it.

Worse was soon to follow. John, in W. L. Warren's words, 'could not resist the temptation to kick a man when he was down'. A victory like that at Mirebeau brought massive temptations in its wake and John succumbed massively. His most serious offence was his responsibility for Arthur's death. (Arthur disappeared, probably murdered, early in April 1203.) The rumours of Arthur's fate soon induced several Norman and Angevin lords with Breton connections to renounce their allegiance to a man they suspected of murdering his nephew. But whatever may or may not have happened to Arthur, the fact is that John's treatment of all the prisoners was widely regarded as being intolerably harsh. According to the *History of William the Marshal* — and as a source for well-informed aristocratic opinion this biography could hardly be bettered — 'he kept his prisoners so vilely and in such evil distress that it seemed shameful and ugly to all those who were with him and who saw this cruelty.'

Since there was hardly a noble in Poitou who did not have a kinsman or friend among the knights captured at Mirebeau, this meant that John managed to offend almost the entire aristocracy, including some who had hitherto steered clear of rebellion. The manner in which John exploited his victory at Mirebeau meant that only six months later he had virtually no friends anywhere in Poitou, Anjou, Maine and Touraine. The last reference to an Angevin seneschal of Anjou is dated 16 April 1203; in this month it was Philip Augustus, not John, who cruised down the Loire and took possession of Saumur. For Philip this was a triumph which simply fell into his lap. Nearly all the work of the conquest of Anjou and northern Poitou was done for him by those whom John had driven into rebellion. Obviously John was not the first Plantagenet ruler to face revolt. Richard indeed had been fatally wounded in a war against rebels, but whereas his troubles were with the nobles of the Limousin and the Angoumois, parts of Aquitaine where ducal authority had always been weak, it was John's special talent to provoke revolt right in the heartland of the Angevin empire.

In diplomacy, John's record was no better. Richard's successes in the war against Philip in the late 1190s had been based on the support of a number of French princes, notably the counts of Flanders, Blois, Boulogne, Perche and Toulouse. John's reasonable showing in 1199 and 1200 owed much to the fact that some of these alliances remained intact for a year or two after Richard's death. But by 1202 there had been a diplomatic revolution. The counts of Boulogne and Toulouse were now in Philip's camp, while the counts of Flanders, Blois and Perche were on their way to the east (the Fourth Crusade). According to Philip's court historian, William the Breton, they had taken the cross once they realized that Richard's death had deprived them of aid and counsel. From John's point of view the breakdown of his brother's carefully cultivated alliances was a disaster.

In the late 1190s Philip had been forced to fight on more than one front. Count Baldwin IX of Flanders, for example, had defeated Philip in 1197 and captured St Omer from him in 1198. Another of Richard's allies, Renaud of Boulogne, had, in the judgement of Philip's biographer, Rigord of St Denis, 'inflicted great damage on the kingdom of France'. However, by 1202, the boot was on the other foot. Baldwin's departure on crusade meant that the Plantagenets had lost a considerable friend — a man impressive enough to be elected as the first Emperor of the Latin Empire of Constantinople — and that Flanders had been neutralized. As for Renaud of Boulogne, during the conquest of Normandy he was to be one of Philip's most distinguished commanders. In the south too, John's diplomacy had faltered. Everyone knew that as soon as Eleanor of Aquitaine died — and she was now more than eighty years old — Gascony would be claimed by King Alfonso VIII of Castile on the plausible grounds that it was his wife's inheritance.

For John to lose the alliance of the Count of Toulouse at this juncture was a serious blow. When Eleanor died, on 1 April 1204, Alfonso's troops were able to march into Gascony almost unopposed. On all fronts John had been outmanoeuvred. This meant that he was faced by a multitude of enemies and was forced to dissipate his resources in order to meet a wide variety of threats. Philip, by contrast, was able to concentrate his forces where and when he chose.

In September 1203 he chose to concentrate on the siege of Château-Gaillard, the great castle which Richard had built at phenomenal speed and enormous expense on the Rock of Andeli on the right bank of the Seine, standing guard over the approaches to Rouen. For over five months of blockade and fierce assault, Château-Gaillard held firm, but eventually, on 6 March 1204, the courageous garrison was compelled to surrender. The castle had come to be seen as the key to Normandy. Its fall had a profound affect on an already low morale. Within three months it was all over. It looks as though a fault in the design of Château-Gaillard's inner citadel may have allowed Philip to make the final assault but, if the defence of Normandy had been competently handled, the French king would never have been allowed to take the two outer wards and thus would never have been in a position even to approach the citadel.

What counted was the fact that throughout the autumn and winter of 1203–4 John made not the slightest effort to relieve the castle or even to harass the blockading French troops. Instead of being treated as one element in a co-ordinated defensive strategy, Château-Gaillard was left to make its own stand against its enemies. Yet even in isolation the castle did its job. By holding the whole military power of the French crown at bay for more than five months, it gained precious time — time which a competent commander would have put to good use. But, on 6 December 1203, John took ship to England and, though he spent time talking about returning to Normandy, it never came to anything more than talk.

Doubtless John felt safer in England. By now he was convinced that the Normans were as 'treacherous' as the Poitevins and Angevins had been. In the opinion of the Barnwell Chronicler, generally regarded as the most judicious of contemporary observers, once John had been deserted by his men, he had little choice but to abandon Normandy. In the final analysis, it was his inability to inspire either affection or loyalty which was fatal. 'No man may ever trust him,' wrote Bertrand de Born the younger, 'for his heart is soft and cowardly.' Teacherous himself, he was always on the lookout for treachery in others. Above all, he feared those of his subjects who, like himself, had been born to wealth and power. His response was to turn away from his barons and rely more and more on his professional soldiers — mercenary captains like Brandin, Martin Algais, Gerard d'Athée and Louvrecaire, all of whom he appointed to high office in 1202 and 1203. 'Why,' asked the biographer of William the

Marshal, 'was John unable to keep the love of his people? It was because Louvrecaire maltreated them and pillaged them as though he were in an enemy's country.'

The *History of William the Marshal* presents us with a picture — amply confirmed from other sources, record sources as well as chronicles — of an obsessively suspicious king:

> When he left Rouen he had his baggage sent on ahead secretly and silently. At Bonneville he stayed the night in the castle, not in the town, for he feared a trap, believing that his barons had sworn to hand him over to the king of France . . . in the morning he slipped away before daybreak while everyone thought he was still asleep.

Who could feel confidence in such a king or wish to fight for him? He was believed to be capable of murdering his nephew, but not of organizing the defence of a beleaguered province. On that belief he foundered.

Not until the Treaty of Paris in 1259 was a Plantagenet king reluctantly prepared to accept the loss of Normandy, Anjou and Poitou. Both John and Henry III made attempts, notably in 1214, 1230 and 1242, to recover their ancestral dominions. But by then they faced an uphill struggle. The 1203–4 transfer of Norman resources from the Plantagenet to the Capetian treasury made an enormous difference to the balance of power. A financial account acquired by the Bibliothèque Nationale shows that by 1221 the ordinary income of the French crown was almost twice what it had been in 1202–3, the date of the earliest surviving set of royal accounts. This meant that the verdict of 1203–4 was, to all intents and purposes, irreversible. From now on the Plantagenets were to be English kings who occasionally visited Ireland and Gascony. Had it not been for John, they might have continued to rule the Angevin empire. There was nothing inevitable about the emergence and survival of the separate national kingdoms of England and France.

CHAPTER IX

ENGLAND AND GASCONY 1216–1337

Robin Studd

HENRY II, RICHARD I AND JOHN were Frenchmen who happened also to become kings of England. Their French territories were their homeland; England merely gave to them their most distinguished title. When Henry III acceded to the throne in 1216, however, so much of the Angevins' French lands had been lost that the political relationship between their territories north and south of the Channel was already beginning to change.

John had been driven out of Normandy by Philip II in 1204. He and his son never gave up hope of recapturing it, but their chances of doing so were sharply reduced by the French king's insistence that their principal subjects, the Anglo-Norman baronage, should choose between their English and French allegiances. For the first time since 1066, the English Channel became a substantial political frontier. Those who settled for England came to identify increasingly with their country of adoption and to see their monarch's commitment to the recovery of his lost territories as a personal rather than a national concern. They could not prevent him from launching a counter-offensive, if he wanted; but they felt no obligation either to participate in person or to support him financially.

One by one the erstwhile Angevin dominions slipped from his grasp. Within twenty years, Anjou, Maine, Touraine and Poitou had gone the way of Normandy, and the young Henry III was left with only the duchy of Gascony in the south-west. This area lay so far from England that the king-dukes could no longer maintain their overlordship as a single political entity as their Norman predecessors had tried to do. Instead, they had to adapt the governmental and administrative machinery to suit the changed political circumstances. The way this was to be done was made clear between 1225 and 1227 when Richard of Cornwall, King Henry's brother, was sent to Gascony at the head of the first expedition to go there since John's reign. Few territories were recaptured; but at least the erosion was halted. And — what was important for the future — Gascony's autonomy was recognized by the elevation of its principal city, Bordeaux, to be the centre of the resident Angevin administration.

The duchy of Gascony which, in broad terms, comprised the area bordered by the Atlantic Ocean, the Pyrenees and the River Garonne, was a particularly distinctive region. It had its own language and its own laws. It was ecclesiastically coterminous with the archdiocese of Auch and, from the tenth century at least, it had its own hereditary counts who, by the eleventh century, were styling themselves dukes. As dukes of Gascony, they acted wholly independently, making treaties, claiming regalian rights and enfeoffing vassals without reference to others. Several subordinate counties were created and in the eleventh century suzerainty was claimed over a number of *vicomtés* (including Béarn) and other lordships which tended to become, in varying degrees, independent themselves in the period following the absorption of the duchy of Gascony into Aquitaine.

This strong tradition of independence and self-governance, which infected the towns too as the communal movement spread to this area in the twelfth century, meant that by the thirteenth century Gascony and the whole region was not easily amenable to political control. Political loyalties were fragile affairs here. Its lords were pliable and prepared to serve those who offered either the greatest reward or else posed the greatest threat, whether from France, Castile, the counts of Toulouse or the Angevins. Allegiances were swapped as convenience dictated so that, throughout his reign prior to the Treaty of Paris of 1259, Henry III's lordship in Gascony was insecure and under continual threat of internal and external attack.

Henry III himself tried twice (in 1230 and 1242) to regain his lost lands and to drive the French from his patrimony by exploiting the feudal difficulties of the French crown, just as it exploited his. In 1230, he took the opportunity of deteriorating relations between Blanche of Castile, the regent of France, and the Bretons and Poitevins to lead his army from St Malo, through Poitou to Bordeaux and back. Although Henry succeeded, albeit briefly, in securing the allegiance of some of the disaffected Poitevin lords, the expedition proved costly, wasteful and politically useless. Even the French remained aloof and, apart from a single siege, there were no battles.

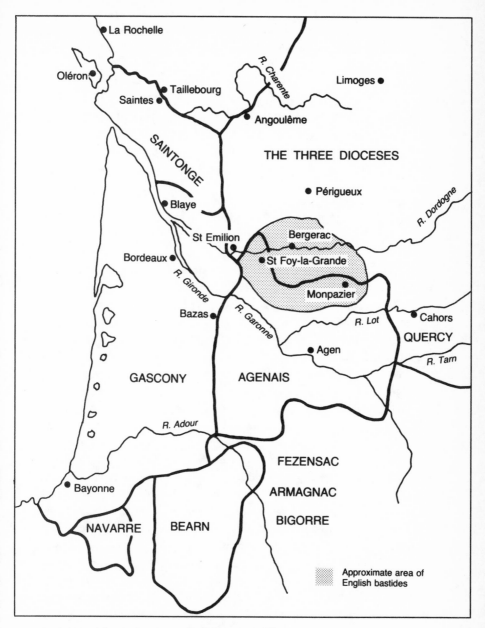

English Gascony c. 1290. Despite the Treaty of Paris agreement in 1259, there was prolonged conflict over English fiefs and domains in the three dioceses of Limoges, Périgueux and Cahors.

In 1242, the Count of La Marche rebelled against his French suzerain and asked for Henry's assistance. The king almost certainly agreed because in 1241 the French king's brother, Alphonse, had been invested with the county of Poitou against the wishes of the local Poitevin lords and in spite of Richard of Cornwall's claim to the county. Henry, however, had problems raising sufficient troops and cash in England, where the barons saw the king's involvement as a private matter. Louis IX, on the other hand, was now better prepared to face the king-duke than he had been twelve years previously. His army mustered at Chinon and, before Henry had landed in the Gironde estuary, rapidly overran the county of La Marche and Poitou. By May 1242, the French had reached the River Charente and threatened Gascony directly. Henry's first encounter with them at Taillebourg was little short of a rout. He withdrew to Saintes, where he was deserted by the Poitevins who had never produced the military and financial support he had expected. The king then retreated in some disarray to Bordeaux where his face was saved by a five-year truce.

It had clearly been an ill-advised campaign, not only because it confirmed the French in their possession of Poitou and northern Saintonge, but also because it contributed to the political crisis which Henry faced on his return to England. His only success was in securing the homage of the Vicomte of Béarn who, in attempting to escape from ties of vassalage to the kingdom of Aragon in order to assert Béarnais independence, was prepared to recognize the suzerainty of the absentee Angevins, and so to return to an allegiance his ancestors had acknowledged until the mid-twelfth century.

This was to be Henry's last opportunity to recover his lost lands by military means. In the 1240s the administrative organization of the duchy was too rudimentary to be able to contain a series of private wars which developed in the Bordelais and elsewhere or to keep mercenary companies out. It was also too thinly stretched to prevent the more distant Pyreneean lords, including the Vicomte of Béarn, from intriguing with the King of Navarre. When the situation demanded a stern hand, the king sent Simon de Montfort to restore order but, as is well known, de Montfort's severity, especially in dealing with the towns, ultimately provoked the civil war he was sent to prevent, so that the king-duke himself, in 1253, and his son Edward, in 1254, had themselves to go to Gascony to deal with the situation. Fortunately for Henry, the King of France was occupied with his crusade but was probably quite content to allow Henry to spend time, money and energy on the pacification of the duchy. There is some evidence too that by the 1250s Louis IX wanted a peaceful settlement of his differences with the Angevins. He was committed to renewing his crusade, and the pope too wished to see their wars concluded.

Yet Henry had certainly lost much ground in France since his accession; Poitou had gone irrevocably and northern Saintonge too. Any influence he might once have had with the dukes of Brittany disappeared when Peter of Dreux did homage to Louis IX in 1236. To the east of Gascony lay the county of Toulouse where ominous political developments were taking place — Alphonse of Poitiers, Louis IX's brother, had married Jeanne, heiress to Raymond VII, Count of Toulouse and, in 1249, became Count of Toulouse as well as Count of Poitou. By the mid-thirteenth century, Gascony was surrounded by loyal vassals of the French crown. Within a year or so, a policy of piecemeal encroachment was being implemented; in 1255 a *bastide* or fortified town was founded at Sainte-Foy-la-Grande, the earliest of a series planted by Alphonse, on the banks of the Dordogne, not forty miles upstream of its confluence with the Garonne and in the disputed area of the Agenais.

It was against this background that negotiations for a peace treaty between Henry III and Louis IX began in 1257. Two years later, on 4 December 1259, the Treaty of Paris was ratified by the two kings in person and its terms were published in Latin and French versions in order to bring them to the widest possible attention.

The most significant of the treaty's clauses made a number of important territorial changes. Louis IX, for example, agreed to surrender his rights in the Three Dioceses (Cahors, Périgueux and Limoges) and, although this sounds as if it was a substantial concession, it was, in fact, far from it. The French king did not hold much territory personally in these bishoprics, and the lands held here by his brother were specifically exempted by the terms of the treaty. What Louis IX did hold were bundles of complex feudal rights of overlordship and it was these that he proposed to surrender. From the outset, this clause proved unworkable and when, in late December 1259, Bertrand de Cardaillac was appointed as seneschal to take custody of these lands for Henry III, he was rebuffed almost everywhere. He also discovered that there were almost no lands to be taken into the king-duke's hands and that the lords of the area were hostile to the suggestion that they should change allegiance in the manner the treaty proposed. In order, therefore, to acquire anything in this area it became necessary for the ducal administration to begin a tiresome process of negotiating terms with each individual lord in turn. This gave rise to many footling disputes on points of detail which dragged on well into Edward I's reign, and some beyond.

It was also agreed in the treaty that the French king would hand over to the English king certain disputed districts which were held by Alphonse of Poitiers and his wife, Jeanne. These included the Agenais (the diocese of Agen) and southern Quercy (the area around Cahors) which had formed part of the dowry provided by Richard I in 1196 for the marriage of his sister Jeanne, with Count Raymond VI of Toulouse, and also southern Saintonge, occupied by the French since 1242 and held by Alphonse as Count of Poitou. The treaty stipulated, however, that the transfer of these territories would take place only if, and when, Alphonse and his wife died without heirs. That looked increasingly likely for their childless marriage had lasted nineteen years and the Count of Poitou was nearly forty, but for the time being it could mean nothing to Henry III. Compensation was offered in the form of a sum of money equivalent to the annual rent of the Agenais, but even the methods by which this was to be assessed were not agreed and provoked a wrangle that went on well into 1261.

The treaty settled little but promised a great deal and in doing so created problems for the future. It was much the same in its attitude to those troublesome southern Gascon lords of Armagnac, Fezensac and Bigorre who claimed independence of the king-duke and who were merely promised an enquiry into their allegiances.

As to the lost Angevin patrimony, Henry agreed to abandon for ever all claims upon the duchy of Normandy and the countries of Anjou, Maine, Touraine and Poitou, and so ratified the annexations of Angevin lands made since 1200. The king renounced his titles to these lands and altered his seal accordingly. From this date onwards, it bore only the legend 'King of England, Lord of Ireland and Duke of Aquitaine'.

In fact, by renouncing his claims on Poitou, Henry agreed to the loss of the greater part of his Aquitanian inheritance. Little more of it than the Aquitanian conquest of the duchy of Gascony remained in his hands. Yet the French king allowed Henry III to keep the title. Why? And why was it not changed to recognize the new political reality?

There was, clearly, much political advantage to the French king to have the English king as his vassal. Considerable prestige was conferred upon the Capetian dynasty by the boast that it numbered a king among its feudatories. The French king was no ordinary monarch, but a king of kings. There was also no question but that the duchy of Aquitaine was, and always had been, an integral part of the kingdom of France and that her dukes had always recognized the French kings' suzerainty and had done homage for their lands. That, hitherto, had not been unequivocably so with the former duchy of Gascony. The French king sought the opportunity to intervene and, so far as possible, to control policy in the remaining Angevin territories. To have permitted the King of England to hold any other title in these circumstances would have denied him that chance. Henry was undoubtedly duped, but was clearly happy enough to retain at least one of his patrimonial titles.

For all his lands south of the Channel, therefore, including Oléron and the Channel Islands and any expectations of land in France that Henry had as a result of the terms of the treaty, he was required to do liege homage, the most restricted and personal form of homage, to the French king. There is no specific mention of the duchy of Aquitaine, but Bordeaux and Bayonne as well as Gascony itself were singled out. For the first time, the duchy of Gascony was explicitly stated to be subject to the suzerainty of the French king and so became as much a part of his kingdom as Berry or the Beauvaisis.

Liege vassals accepted that their homage took precedence over all other feudal relationships. Liege homage imposed several important limitations on the vassal's capacity for independent action. For Henry III, the consequences of his entering into this contract were, as for any liege vassal, a requirement to provide military service, in person if summoned, general obedience and exclusive support in his suzerain's political quarrels, and a duty to attend his court and to sit in judgement as a peer of France and as Duke of Aquitaine. The scope for embarrassment was enormous.

For Gascony, however, the treaty had the effect of superimposing a higher tier of authority above and beyond that of the king-duke. The highest court of the King of France, the Parlement of Paris, therefore became the ultimate court of appeal for Gascons as for other Frenchmen. Time and again during the next eighty years, French monarchs used this situation to their advantage to make perfectly peaceful and legal inroads into the remaining authority of the Angevins in France. Henry laid his dominions in France open to all the ingenuity of the French lawyers and to all the pertinacity of the French royal officials in the region. Within two or three weeks of the ratification of the treaty, Renaud de Pons and Marguerite de Turenne had appealed against an unfavourable decision in the Gascon courts on their claim to the succession to the lordship of Bergerac. They set a precedent, but it was followed by many Gascons who had exhausted legal process in the duchy itself. In one four-year period, 1274–8, no less than thirty Gascon appeals are known to have been before the Parlement. By the simple application of feudal law and without recourse to war, the French crown could whittle away what remained of Angevin authority and integrate their dominions fully within the kingdom of France. In the 1290s, Edward I tried to divert Gascon appeals to the royal courts in London but to no avail, and he found himself compelled to adopt a defensive policy in his own duchy of giving as little cause for French intervention in its affairs as possible.

For England, the consequences of the treaty were similarly far-reaching. The rump of Angevin lands left in France had, ever since 1214, been of less importance than the lands to the north of the Channel. Instead of an itinerant monarch attempting to rule from whatever part of the Angevin teritories he happened to be in, the king now established Westminster as his seat of government and ruled Gascony through an officer with quasi-regal powers. Royal absences from England, normal before 1214, became exceptional. After the ratification of the treaty, Henry never went back to the duchy. But already, and initially in response to the demands of the Gascon townsmen, Henry had attempted to redefine the constitutional relationship between the duchy and the English crown. In February 1254, he conferred an appanage upon his elder son, the future Edward I, and granted him, among other places, all the remaining territories of the Crown in France — Gascony, Oléron and the Channel Islands — which he was to hold on such terms 'that they should never be separated from the crown . . . but should remain to the kings of England in their entirety for ever'. Gascony ceased, from this moment, to be the private property of the king and was formally annexed to the English crown. The king, with Edward exercising the lordship, now saw his relationship to his Gascon subjects in much the same terms as he viewed his English subjects. It was not a view to which the French crown was prepared to give credence, but it was one which the Gascons, particularly the townsmen, accepted.

Maintaining his rule in Gascony was a costly business for Henry III. For instance, from the 1220s onwards, the Gascon towns were provided with money to build, rebuild and repair their ramparts. After the departure of the French in 1228, new castles were built (the donjon of St Emilion, for instance) and others were bought by the king in order to make the defence of the duchy more effective, although there were never enough for the task. Alliances also had to be purchased and privileges conceded; both could be costly. From 1224, Gascony was certainly a drain on royal resources and one wonders why, given the insecurity of his tenure of these territories, Henry did not abandon them altogether. Such a course of action is unlikely to have occurred to him. No man in the Middle Ages abandoned his patrimony as easily as that. To do so would have been contrary to family honour and alien to the spirit of the age. There were also many in the duchy, particularly the townsmen, whose political support had been courted ever since John's reign, who supported and encouraged the Angevins, preferring English to French overlordship. Moreover, there was an important practical considera-tion: given the right peaceful circumstances, Gascony could become a profitable asset.

The economic development of Gascony would not have been possible but for the administrative arrangements made during Henry III's reign. Until 1224, separate seneschals were appointed as principal executive officers for each of the constituent parts of the duchy of Aquitaine-Poitou, Gascony, Limousin and Périgord. From 1227, however, and as a result of changes made while Richard of Cornwall was in Gascony, a single seneschal, the Seneschal of Gascony, emerged as the principal officer for all the king-duke's lands in the region. To begin with, he appears to have had comprehensive powers in every sphere of the administration, but gradually, as is a common theme of thirteenth-century administrative history, particular duties were delegated to others. In 1242–3 a financial officer was appointed to collect the revenues of Gascony and of the island of Oléron, and a treasury was established in the abbey of Sainte-Croix of Bordeaux. In 1254, the treasury was moved to the castle of the Ombrière in Bordeaux and its castellan, the Constable of Bordeaux, became the financial officer of the duchy. A controller to assist the constable and to supervise the customs revenue was introduced during the reign of Edward I. A council of Gascons to advise and assist the seneschal, whose duties required a detailed knowledge of Gascon custom, is known to have operated from at least 1245. A system of courts to hear complaints against local officials is first recorded in 1255, as is the earliest reference to an official seal. A sub-seneschal first occurs in 1272 and indicates the growing volume and sophistication of the seneschal's responsibilities. By 1289, when Edward I issued his ordinances for the administration of Gascony, sub-seneschals were appointed for each of the Gascon *pays*, and a staff of judges, proctors, receivers, *baillis*, and clerks had precisely defined duties to fulfil.

It was a centralized system of administration but, in general, it worked and, because Gascons were not excluded from any office, it was accepted. There were occasional problems concerning individual office-holders but no more than elsewhere, and the king-duke's writ ran more effectively in this century than at any other period. Through his officials, Edward I was able directly to control the minting of the local *bordelais* money. Through them he set out to improve navigation on the lesser rivers, such as the Isle and the Dropt, and, in the *Haut-Pays*, on the more substantial Tarn and Lot, in order to facilitate the passage of wine barges downstream to Bordeaux. In the 1270s and 1280s, the king-duke's officers were ordered to construct *bastides* throughout the duchy, especially in the Agenais which the French finally ceded in 1279. About 140 *bastides* were planned by Edward and about 100 were built in order to secure the newly acquired areas politically and, equally significantly, to permit them to be exploited economically. As far as possible, Gascony had to be made to pay. Both Henry III and Edward I set out to see that it did.

Wine was, of course, Gascony's greatest resource. After the loss of La Rochelle, the Gascon vineyard developed swiftly; its wines became as familiar in England as the wines of Aunis and Poitou had been before. Bordeaux was conveniently situated to take the advantage. It was on the Gironde estuary and close to the confluence of the Garonne and the Dordogne, the two great rivers of the duchy which, with their tributaries, drained its hinterland. It rapidly acquired a monopoly control of the entire Gascon trade, as well as being the port through which imports of cereals, cloth, wood, salt-fish and other commodities passed to meet Gascon needs as its own economy became a monoculture.

The king-duke benefited considerably from this commercial activity, in particular from his ability to levy customs duties on all goods entering or leaving the Gironde. The customs of Bordeaux accounted for more than a third of the total income of the duchy in 1306–7, according to the earliest surviving constable's account. It is likely, however, that this proportion of the total revenue was at least as high in the later thirteenth century and that the total volume exported in the early fourteenth century, between 90,000 and 100,000 tons a year was reached, and probably exceeded, in the years before the French invasion of 1294.

These trading links also had political implications for they gave others besides the king-duke a stake in the fortunes of the duchy. They made many Gascon and English merchants extremely wealthy and went some way towards compensating for the lack of a landed connection between England and the duchy. They certainly drew the remaining Angevin dominions into a close interdependence and provided the Gascons and the king-duke with powerful reasons for wishing to preserve the political links between them and a common interest in resisting the French.

However, by the terms of the Treaty of Paris, liege homage was required of the king-duke at each change of lord and vassal. Following the deaths of Louis IX and Henry III, Edward I was required to recognize the suzerainty of Philip III. He did so at Paris on 6 August 1273, but in a form, 'Lord King, I do you homage, thus, for all the lands which I ought to hold of you', which indicates both that he was seeking to avoid the suppressive form of the contract that Henry III had agreed to in 1259, and that he expected the French to implement the treaty in full. Philip III's refusal to surrender the former lands of Alphonse of Poitiers, who had died childless in 1271, precipitated a sharp deterioration in relations between the king-duke and his suzerain as it rapidly became obvious that the new French king regarded the treaty of 1259 as but a postponement of the war of conquest of the Angevin dominions.

Try as they might, for eighty years after 1259, English kings found no satisfactory way of extricating themselves from the consequences of Henry III's unguarded concession. Twice, in 1294 and 1324, Gascony was declared forfeit to the French crown on some flimsy pretext, and invaded and conquered. Twice, and for different reasons, it was restored to English kings who were anxious to preserve the commercial links between England and Gascony. By 1337, however, they had had enough. When, for the third time, the duchy was confiscated, Edward III, intending revenge, stood firm and the Hundred Years War began.

CHAPTER X

BEFORE THE ARMADA: IBERIA AND ENGLAND IN THE MIDDLE AGES

Anthony Goodman

THE POLITICAL AND CULTURAL PROFILES of medieval Spain started to emerge with clarity in the last decades of the eleventh century. The collapse after 1008 of the powerful Muslim caliphate of Córdoba and the fragmentation by 1031 of Moorish Spain (al-Andalus) into competing successor-states facilitated the independence, enrichment and expansion of the caliphate's former Christian satellite principalities to the north at the expense of the Moors. These principalities, in order to strengthen and reconstruct their societies, sought integration with a revived western Christendom, which was now able and willing to supply surplus manpower, specialist military expertise, the alliance of powerful kings and a reformist religious ideology — one novel component of which was crusading. In the twelfth century, convergent Iberian and northern European interests created the first significant and enduring links between the Peninsula and England. According to Derek Lomax, St Godric of Finchale, County Durham, is the first English pilgrim known to have visited the shrine of St James at Compostela in Galicia; this was before 1110, probably in 1102. In 1147, significantly, English crusaders assisted in the siege of Lisbon and its capture from the Moors.

Santiago de Compostela became one of the most popular foreign shrines in medieval England. A burial in Worcester Cathedral excavated in 1986 contained a body in pilgrim garb, including the cockleshell, the pilgrim badge associated with Santiago. In the later fourteenth century, war between England and Castile (of which Galicia was part) did not dim this English enthusiasm. The typical pilgrim described then by the popular poet William Langland had 'shelles of Galice' among the badges in his hat; in 1417, Margery Kempe, burgess's wife of King's Lynn, Norfolk, embarked thither with a boatload of pilgrims at Bristol. This was an intrepid undertaking since her fellow pilgrims, alarmed by her extravagant displays of devotion, threatened to throw her overboard if there was a storm. Fortunately, the sailing weather was calm.

Langland's contemporary, the courtly poet Geoffrey Chaucer, reflected enthusiasm in noble circles for the reconquest, *Reconquista*, of the remaining fragment of Muslim Spain, the kingdom of Granada. He says of the Knight, in the Prologue to *The Canterbury Tales*: 'In Gernade [Granada] at the sege eek hadde he be / Of Algezir'. Alfonso XI of Castile had commenced the siege of Algeciras in 1342 and in the following year he was joined there by Henry of Grosmont, future Duke of Lancaster, the flower of English chivalry, and by the Earl of Salisbury. It was a siege which was to establish the Lancastrian family's continuing interest in crusading in Spain: Grosmont's grandson Bolingbroke, soon to be Henry IV, was urged to revive the crusade against Granada in 1398 and his son Thomas Duke of Clarence tried to do so in 1412.

Returning to the latter half of the twelfth century, we find a quickening Anglo-Norman interest in Spanish affairs reflected in chronicles such as those of Roger Howden and Robert of Torigny as well as in royal policies. Torigny noted stirring episodes in the *Reconquista* and explained that since Alfonso VII ruled over the petty kings of Aragon and Galicia, he was entitled 'Emperor of Spain'. The Angevin kings of England, in their capacity as dukes of Aquitaine, were neighbours of Navarre and Aragon and were consequently drawn into Spanish politics. In 1176, Henry II of England married his daughter Eleanor to Alfonso VIII of Castile and in 1191 Richard the Lionheart married Berengaria, daughter of Sancho VI of Navarre. Soon after the martyrdom of St Thomas of Canterbury, Eleanor introduced his cult into Castile; with her husband, she refounded the convent of Las Huelgas near Burgos, where the couple's kneeling effigies can be seen over their tomb.

It was at Las Huelgas that the most important Anglo-Spanish marriage of the early Middle Ages was celebrated: there, in 1254, Henry III's son, the future Edward I, married Alfonso X's sister Eleanor, both bride and groom being in their teens. This important marriage alliance showed how English perceptions of Spain had altered in the decades after the decisive victory of the Christian kings over the Moors at Las Navas de Tolosa in 1212. The *Reconquista* by Castile and Aragon, gathering pace from the 1230s, made them undisputedly the great powers of the Iberian Peninsula, eclipsing Granada, Navarre and even Portugal, whose status as a kingdom had been recognized by the papacy in 1185 and whose size was vastly extended to include Moorish Algarve. In English eyes, the *Reconquista* confirmed the pre-eminence of Castile. Her kings were commonly referred to in England throughout the Middle Ages as kings of Spain, and with good reason: their realm contained the ancient metropolitan see of Toledo and the body of the Apostle James; and their nobility was famed for its strong crusading ethos which was nourished and stimulated by the long Castilian land frontier with Islam.

One consequence of the rise of Castile and Aragon in the early thirteenth century was that their kings flexed their muscles more widely in Christendom. Matthew Paris, a monk of St Albans, though he did not know Fernando III of Castile's name, did know that he was a great crusading hero in the Peninsula and knew about his embassy to Henry III, probably in 1251. Fernando's knight told Henry that since his master had captured Seville from the Moors in 1248, 'almost all Spain as far as the sea-coast' had submitted to his authority. In the light of the recent failure in Egypt of Louis IX of France's crusade, the knight put the proposal to Henry that he should go to Spain in order to join Fernando in a crusade to free Jerusalem. In effect, the suggestion was that Henry should help Castile to assert the leadership of Christendom in place of the French. The proposal was dashed by Fernando's death in 1252 and his son Alfonso X's different policy — he had designs on Henry's duchy of Aquitaine.

The confrontation over the duchy, however, was soon resolved: the Treaty of Toledo in 1254 was intended as a comprehensive settlement between Alfonso and Henry, binding them and their successors in a close family alliance. One provision was that Henry would seek to participate in a crusade in Morocco or elsewhere in Africa — but he was principally concerned to neutralize the Castilian threat to Gascony and, apart from the marriage of Edward and Eleanor, neglected to fulfil other treaty provisions, to Alfonso's annoyance. Yet the alliance quickened the pace of Anglo-Iberian contacts. In the 1250s, Henry III patronized Alfonso X's brothers with characteristic generosity, promising Felipe rich ecclesiastical benefices in England, entertaining Sancho lavishly and maintaining the disgraced Enrique, who was licensed to take royal deer at Havering Park in Essex. Spanish entertainers appeared at court: in 1255, Henry rewarded two of Alfonso's *istriones*, players, with gifts of twenty shillings apiece. The king's generosity to Spaniards offended English xenophobia, which was growing apace throughout this period. According to Matthew

Paris, the habits of Sancho and his household evoked astonishment and disgust:

> The manner, habits and attendants of this bishop elect [of Toledo] entirely differed from those amongst us; for he was a young man, wore a ring on his forefinger, and gave a blessing to the people. He ornamented his place of abode, which was at the New Temple [London], and even the floor of it, with tapestries, palls and curtains; yet he had a vulgar and extraordinary body of attendants, and only kept a few palfreys, though he had a great many mules . . . the citizens of London, on finding out their customs and manners, abused and insulted them, taunting them with gluttony and luxuriousness.

Matthew Paris also relates that superior Spanish standards of domestic comfort and refinement, introduced by Edward's wife Eleanor, excited similar reactions of disapproving wonder:

> When Eleanor arrived at the place of abode assigned to her, she found it, like the dwelling of the bishop elect of Toledo, hung with palls of silk and tapestry, like a temple, and even the floor was covered with arras. This was done by the Spaniards, it being in accordance with the custom of their country; but this excessive pride excited the laughter and derision of the people.

Later in life, when she was Edward I's queen (1272–90), Eleanor retained a nostalgic taste for her native fruits and for southern artefacts. From a Spanish ship, docked at Plymouth, she purchased figs, raisins, dates, pomegranates, lemons and oranges, as well as Venetian glass and Moorish majolica. These princely examples of semi-Moresque households in thirteenth-century England may have helped to stimulate the growing enthusiasm of English nobles for conspicuous consumption, especially their craving for Mediterranean delicacies and craftware. Castile and, to a lesser extent, Portugal, after the conquests in the rich Moorish south, were well placed to cater for their demands. The ports of the Bay of Biscay, such as Santander and San Sebastián, thrived on this trade, which, as Wendy Childs has shown, reached peaks in the 1320s and 1330s. Not all Spanish imports were welcome: William Rishanger, another chronicler of St Albans, claimed that the disease which spread among English flocks in 1274 was widely attributed to infection from a Spanish sheep imported into Northumberland.

The Anglo-Castilian treaty of 1254 helped trade, for it provided an amicable basis for the settlement of disputes arising from acts of piracy and the official detention of ships and cargoes. The reign of Edward I (1272–1307) was the high noon of Anglo-Spanish political relations in the Middle Ages, though not entirely unclouded. Edward cultivated close ties with the leading Iberian powers. As one who had crusaded in the Mediterranean, he appreciated the extent of Aragonese power there. His correspondence with his brother-in-law, Alfonso X of Castile, who had knighted him many years before at Las Huelgas and after whom one of his sons had been named, bears witness to their mutual respect and affection. Moreover, Edward had a genuine love for his Spanish queen, who bore him fourteen or so children.

As queen, Eleanor was a harsh landowner; her officials were denounced by Archbishop Pecham of Canterbury as 'of the stock of the devil rather than of Christ'. Visiting her manor of Havering, she imperiously ordered peasants, who had the temerity to behave recalcitrantly in her presence, to be imprisoned with nothing but rushes to lie on. After three days and nights, they were more amenable. She then ordered that her tenants there should go weaponless and leash their dogs when passing the locally controversial warren she had had made. Nevertheless, Queen Eleanor, who had come to surround herself with English clerks and had developed Anglo-French literary tastes, accomplished the rare feat, for a foreign medieval queen, of being popular with the touchy English in general. The panegyric on her by the sixteenth-century chronicler, Raphael Holinshed, echoes the obituary notice of her contemporary Rishanger: 'She was a goodly and modest princess full of pity, and one that showed much favour to the English nation, ready to relieve every man's grief that sustained wrong, and to make them friends that were at discord.'

Holinshed went on to mention Edward I's erection of the 'Eleanor Crosses' — twelve elaborate and very expensive stone crosses set up during the 1290s at the places where her funeral cortège had halted on its procession from Harby in Nottinghamshire to her principal burial place in Westminster Abbey (her heart and viscera were accorded their own shrines in the London Dominican house (Blackfriars) and Lincoln cathedral respectively). Three of the original crosses, remarkably, survive — at Geddington and Hardingstone in Northamptonshire and at Waltham in Hertfordshire. However, the ones which were nationally famous in late medieval and early modern England, and which Holinshed singled out, were the particularly imposing London crosses, the cross within the city, in Cheapside, and Charing Cross. The latter was erected on the way to the royal palace at Westminster and stood at the Trafalgar Square end of what is now Whitehall, not on the site of its modern (1863) replacement. Cheapside Cross was the more famous of the two, being on the city's main processional route. It was also one of the principal features decorated for pageant receptions, such as that accorded to Henry V after his victory at Agincourt in 1415 and to Catherine of Aragon as the bride of Arthur Prince of Wales in 1501. This cross was demolished in 1643, as was that at Charing Cross four years later. The two had become symbols which were politically and, even more so, religiously, unacceptable to the new parliamentary regime. However, hitherto they had been a unique and inescapable reminder of the Spanish descent of Edward I's successors and of the importance of Anglo-Spanish relations. Their erection marked a high point in that relationship; its deterioration under Edward's descendants was to be significantly reversed much later, under the early Tudors.

It was characteristic of the limited horizons of Eleanor of Castile's son Edward II, who reigned from 1307 to 1327 — the only medieval English king with a Spanish parent — that he took only a perfunctory interest in Iberian affairs, until war with the French crown over his duchy of Gascony (1323–5) galvanized him into seeking allies in the Peninsula. In contrast, his son and successor Edward III (d. 1377) valued his Spanish descent and strenuously sought Peninsular alliances, particularly that of Castile, in order to weaken his French opponents in the first phases of the Hundred Years War and bolster the security of the duchy of Gascony. With Edward's endorsement, in 1366, his eldest son the Black Prince initiated a policy of military intervention in Castile, in which two of Edward's younger sons, John of Gaunt, Duke of Lancaster, and Edmund of Langley, Earl of Cambridge, were to be heavily involved. The principal aim of Edward and his sons — to gain the alliance of Castile against the French crown — was pursued well into the reign of Richard II. However, it was to end in utter failure. In 1369, Henry II of Castile became a close ally of the French; his successors stuck to this alliance and provided significant naval and military support against the English, most intensively in the two decades before the truces of 1389. This 'twenty years' war' badly damaged Anglo-Castilian trade and produced long-lasting feelings of hostility: a formal peace was ratified only in 1467.

The first official English military intervention occurred in 1367, when the Black Prince and his brother John of Gaunt invaded Castile from their Gascon bases, going through the pass of Roncesvalles and the kingdom of Navarre. The prince's aim was to restore the tyrannical Pedro I to his throne, from which he had been expelled by his illegitimate half-brother Henry of Trastamara (the future Henry II). At Nájera, the Black Prince won a famous victory over Henry and the French mercenary companies supporting him. Shortly after Pedro's triumphant entry into Burgos, the Black Prince arrived there, staying at the convent of Las Huelgas, so closely associated with his family's history. But the prince had backed the wrong horse: Pedro proved an unreliable ally and, in 1369, he was captured, killed and usurped by his grim and forceful brother Henry.

Edward's riposte to Henry's coup was to marry his son, John of Gaunt, to Pedro's refugee daughter and heiress Constance and to recognize Gaunt as King of Castile in the right of his bride (1371–2). As Duke of Lancaster, Gaunt was the richest English landowner; in his early thirties, proved in the battle at Nájera, his was a forceful personality, genial and irascible, sententious and often shrewd, munificent and ambitious. He was intensely loyal to the Plantagenet family interest and, as befitted the pretender to the Castilian throne, had a high concept of royal authority. He used seals appropriate to his royal office and had a Castilian chancery which employed the correct forms. He was supportive towards those of Pedro's adherents who fled to England in the early 1370s and a few Spaniards rose high in his service. But the personnel and culture of his court remained Anglo-French: he apparently had little admiration for anything Spanish, except the cult of Santiago, the crusading tradition (much decayed, in English eyes) and horse-harness. By presenting his intended expedition to Castile in 1386 as a crusade against the schismatic adherents of the antipope, he attempted to whip up English fervour against Spaniards. However, Gaunt was so unpopular domestically in the early part of his nephew Richard II's reign that had he appeared to be a hispanophile, Spaniards would have been an object of popular fury. His queen, the impassioned and devout Constance, evoked sympathies because his neglect of her was another stick with which he could be beaten.

In support of the war against Castile, English forces operated in Portugal in 1372, in Navarre in 1378–9 and in Portugal again in 1381–2 and 1385: the interventionist phase ended with Gaunt's occupation of much of Galicia in 1386 and his joint invasion of León in 1387 with John I of Portugal. However, Henry II of Castile, who died in 1379, had managed some shrewd blows against the English. In 1372, his galley-fleet struck a decisive blow against English rule in Aquitaine by annihilating off La Rochelle a force under the command of the incoming royal lieutenant, the fiery young Earl of Pembroke. As Pembroke lay in his Spanish gaol, he was upbraided by a Welsh captain, Owain Lawgoch ('of the Red Hand'), who claimed to be the rightful Prince of Wales. In 1377, Henry II prepared to back Owain's claim with a Spanish invasion of Wales, a plan that so alarmed the English government that it speedily garrisoned key Welsh castles. However, Henry II opted for a more direct strategy: he initiated a series of summer attacks by his galley-fleet in co-operation with the French, on southern English coasts. In 1377, for instance, Rye, Lewes, Portsmouth, Dartmouth and Plymouth were sacked and the Isle of Wight was overrun.

The climax of the Anglo-Castilian war came in 1386–7. Gaunt and Constance sailed from Plymouth, middle-aged adventurers hoping either to defeat Henry II's less self-assured son John I in battle or to make a final settlement, by marrying their one child, Catherine, to his son and heir, thus effecting an Anglo-Castilian peace. At first they triumphed: Galician towns submitted to their allegiance and Santiago was restored to the Roman obedience with the installation of a new bishop. However, with the conquest of Galicia in 1386, Gaunt had shot his bolt; his small army began to waste alarmingly from disease and he had no hope of substantial reinforcements or additional finance. Negotiations with John I for a marriage settlement broke down: John coolly concluded that he could safely allow the English to occupy remote and mountainous Galicia. The English, used to travelling there on pilgrimage, seem to have overestimated its strategic importance and the psychological impact of their winning over of Santiago. In 1387, Gaunt could put only a token force into the field for what was essentially a Portuguese invasion of León. A Franco-Castilian defence system superior to Portuguese siege-craft, heat and epidemic disease which drained the willpower of Gaunt and his men, as well as the absence of native support for his claim, led to a rapid curtailment of the campaign, which had degenerated into a hunt for victuals and fodder. Nevertheless, soon after the crestfallen Gaunt had re-entered Portugal, John I of Castile threw him an unexpected lifeline — soaring war costs were making him desperate for a settlement rather than a pursuit. Most of the terms were rapidly agreed, and by the final version, the Treaty of Bayonne in 1388, Gaunt and Constance relinquished their claims on the crown of Castile and recognized John's title to it. In return, they received heavy financial compensations and the marriage soon afterwards of their daughter Catherine to John's son and heir Henry. That year the young couple were created Prince and Princess of Asturias; for the first time, Asturias was granted as a principality to the heir of the Castilian throne. This development was doubtless an imitation of the role of the principality of Wales; it was by his title to Wales that Gaunt's brother, the Black Prince, had been generally known in Spain. Though documentary proof is lacking, it is likely that the endowment of the Castilian heir with a principality was made at Gaunt's suggestion, as a means of reflecting honour on his daughter as well as on the house of Trastamara.

There is some slight evidence that Galicia rather than Asturias had been discussed as a principality for Prince Henry and his bride Catalina; this would have suited Gaunt better, salving his pride at having to give up Galicia under the treaty terms and providing opportunities for him to exert some family interest in a province hallowed in English eyes. Any further exertion of Lancastrian influence, however, was unwelcome in Castilian governing circles. Even before the untimely death of John I of Castile in 1390, with whom Gaunt had struck up a congenial relationship, Gaunt's plans to effect an Anglo-Castilian peace had been dashed, and his further initiatives during the reign of his son-in-law Henry III (d. 1406) were frozen out. Doubtless, levies to pay the large annual indemnity due to Gaunt under the treaty terms until his death in 1399 did not endear him and his countrymen in Castile. His daughter, Catalina of Lancaster (d. 1416), who acted as co-regent for her son John II during his minority, had to tread carefully not to appear anglophile.

The war had stimulated a sense of national antagonism, though on the English side this was tempered by reverence for Santiago and, in noble circles, nostalgia for the crusade against Granada. War propaganda is evident in the speech of John I to the Cortes in 1386. God had marked the English physically and popes had imposed levies on them, he said, so that their sins would always remain in the memory of men. John was alluding to the legend that Englishmen had tails and to the ancient papal tax known as Peter's Pence. The English, he went on, had commonly rebelled against the Church, killing St Thomas of Canterbury and making other martyrs. They had always favoured unjust wars, not fearing God or caring about anything except to carry off spoils with pride and haughtiness. In his explanation of the national characteristics of the English, King John was perhaps catering for the historical tastes of the better educated in his audience. In a chivalrous biography, *El Vitorial*, written in the 1430s, the Castilian noble Gutierre Díaz de Gamez provides historical reasons among others for what he sees as the uniquely unpleasant and aggressive character of the English. Their forebears, Trojans led by Brutus, had conquered the giants who originally inhabited the island and married their daughters, inheriting a perverse behavioural strain from the giant race. Díaz de Gamez was clearly acquainted, either through Geoffrey of Monmouth's twelfth-century work or romances which derived from it, with the legendary history of Britain, which culminated in the deeds of King Arthur.

Chivalrous romances about the supposed English past and the chivalrous reputation of the English court and nobility (as embodied, for instance, in the Order of the Garter) had attractions for the Iberian nobility in the fifteenth century, despite the sourness of Díaz de Gamez. Spanish knights performed feats of arms before the court of Henry VI of England. One knight, Joanot Martorell, a noble of Valencia in the kingdom of Aragon, persuaded the youthful Henry to act as umpire in a dispute of honour with a fellow Valencian in 1438. It was probably while in England in 1438–9 that Martorell composed a romance, *Guillem de Varoych*, based on a version of the Anglo-Norman romance about the mythical Guy of Warwick. This was the family legend of the earls of Warwick: Martorell gave his hero some of the characteristics of Richard Beauchamp, Earl of Warwick (d. 1439), who had been in charge of Henry VI's upbringing and was internationally renowned for his chivalry. Martorell also inserted a racy account of the origins of the Order of the Garter. Castilian nobles too could be impressed by the English court culture and English legends. Diego de Valera, a knightly follower of John II of Castile, visited England in 1442 and was honourably entertained by his master's kinsmen. Valera recorded how he went to Greenwich, the home of John's cousin Humphrey of Gloucester, and saw the duke wearing his ceremonial robes on an important feast-day, as did two Castilian heralds. Valera also witnessed the elevation in the peerage of Henry VI's leading kinsmen John and Edmund Beaufort. In one of his historical works, Valera said that there existed in one part of England barnacle geese born of the fruit of trees (a well-known medieval legend). He had asked the Cardinal of England (Henry Beaufort, the late Catalina's half-brother) about this: the cardinal had affirmed its truth.

According to Díaz de Gamez, England was a land of marvels, full of serpents and dragons, and home to men wholly covered in hair who drank from mountain streams. Such trust in myths does not suggest that the Castilian nobility knew much about England outside its court, except what they read in romances and absorbed from travellers' tales. We may contrast the intimate knowledge of many parts of Spain gained by English knights, especially in the later fourteenth century; the chronicler John Froissart recorded some of their unpleasant recollections of its bleaker and more parched landscapes. No Spaniard established himself as an English lord in the later Middle Ages, whereas there were a few English mercenary captains who received land grants in Spain — notably, in the late 1360s, the renowned Cheshire knight Hugh Calveley who, for his services to the Aragonese crown received castles in Valencia and the hand in marriage of the heiress to a Catalan barony; unfortunately, the marriage broke down.

There was a Portuguese lady who was prominent in early fifteenth-century England — Beatrice, illegitimate daughter of John I of Portugal. It was on her request that Henry IV of England procured her marriage to the Earl of Arundel in 1405. She subsequently married John Holand, Earl of Huntingdon, a close kinsman of the Lancastrian dynasty; she died in 1439. Her magnificent effigy can be seen with her first husband's in the FitzAlan Chapel at Arundel in Sussex; as can the brass of her principal lady, Agnes, who was Portuguese and who married an Englishman, Thomas Salmon, an esquire of Henry V. Other prominent personnel of Countess Beatrice's household at Arundel Castle were Portuguese: she continued to maintain links with her father's court.

Portugal was the one part of the Peninsula where English economic, political and cultural links were assiduously cultivated in the first half of the fifteenth century. In 1385, English archers had helped to preserve Portuguese independence at the battle of Aljubarrota, where a Castilian army was decisively defeated by John I (d. 1433), first king of the house of Avis. The following year, he made the defence treaty with Richard II, the Treaty of Windsor, which has often been invoked, down to the present century. In 1387, King John married Gaunt's daughter Philippa as part of their new personal alliance. The accession of her brother Henry IV to the English throne in 1399, as already seen, strengthened the links between the royal dynasties. This further facilitated a thriving trading relationship, which had in part resulted from the displacement of direct Anglo-Castilian trade. An English political polemicist of 1436 wrote approvingly about this commerce:

Portuguese with us have truth in hand,
Whose merchandise comes much into England.
They be our friends with their commodities,
And we English pass into their countries.
Her land has oil, wine, osey [a type of wine], wax and grain,
Figs, raisins, honey and cordweine [ornamented leather from Córdoba in
    Castile],
Dates and salt, hides and such merchandise.

The Portuguese court was eager to emulate the English — for instance, in the reorganization of its chapel royal in the 1440s. Portugal was then ruled by a regent, Dom Pedro, Duke of Coimbra, one of the sons of Philippa of Lancaster. Her sons considered themselves Lancastrian princes but the most famous of them all was Prince Henry the Navigator (d. 1460). When their father John had gone on crusade with them in 1415 and captured Ceuta in Morocco, they were probably more directly inspired by the crusading traditions of the house of Lancaster than by the earlier Portuguese crusading traditions: in the 1390s Lancastrian crusading had been revived by Gaunt's sons, the future Henry IV and John Beaufort. Such examples probably also helped to stimulate Henry the Navigator's encouragement of voyages down the coast of Africa, aimed at undermining the Moors by diverting the sources of their wealth — and also enabling Henry to pursue a princely lifestyle comparable to that of his English kinsfolk.

There was rejoicing in England at the capture of Ceuta, whereas the occupation of the Canary Islands by the Spaniards in 1404 had been dismissed there as profiteering by the enslavement of natives. The fading in England of the crusading image of Castile overlapped with more widespread disillusion with the ideals of a united Christendom, as a result of the Great Schim (1378–1419), the failure to organize an effective crusade to stem the Turkish advances, the revival of heresies and despondency over the attempts of general councils of the Church to reform it in the early fifteenth century. Such failures and divisions were compounded, and in some instances worsened, by the emergence of more clearly defined and assertive nation-states, particularly in the crucible of the Hundred Years War. Common cultural ideals and interests which had enabled nobilities in different parts of western Christendom to empathize with each other and to identify common aims were weakened, or in some cases reinterpreted to foster national feeling. As seen in the Anglo-Castilian confrontations — an element in the Hundred Years War — a component in the development of national states was the making and dissemination of a hostile collective profile of opponents, sometimes using information drawn from legendary histories and about saintly cults which were part of the common culture of western Christendom.

Nevertheless, fragments of common culture and purpose lingered on in the fifteenth century among the western nobilities, enshrined especially in the courtly codes of chivalry and in the world of international tournaments and secular orders of chivalry. Such links facilitated some mending of Anglo-Castilian relations. In contrast, the reception in Portugal of these newly elaborated courtly behavioural modes helped to create the dynamic for a nation-state which expanded in a wholly unexpected way. The house of Avis developed a renovated image and role for Portuguese royalty, by adopting institutions, mores and aspirations derived from the mainstream of courtly culture. This largely resulted from the new English connection. In this respect, as in some others, the English unwittingly became godfathers to the first European overseas empire.

CHAPTER XI

THE FAILURE OF THE FIRST BRITISH EMPIRE?

England's Relations with Ireland, Scotland and Wales 1066–1500

R. R. Davies

'EDWARD THE GREAT, KING OF ENGLAND, Wales and Scotland, Duke of Gascony and Lord of Ireland died.' It was with these words that an Irish annalist recorded the death of Edward I in 1307. Technically, his obituary notice could be faulted, since he ascribed to Edward titles he did not assume (King of Wales and Scotland); but substantively it was correct. It registered the opinion, shared by other contemporaries, that Edward was not only King of England but also in effect ruler of the British Isles. The evidence was obvious and incontrovertible: Edward had conquered north and west Wales, thereby bringing the whole country under English control; he was Lord of Ireland and his governmental and judicial authority there extended even to the furthest districts of the south-west; by 1305, he had secured the submission of almost all the leaders of the political community of Scotland and had prepared an ordinance for the government of the country under his rule. Such a king surely deserved the accolade of 'the Great' and fully justified contemporary comparisons of his achievements with those of King Arthur.

How was it that the 'King of the English' of 1066 had been transformed, in effect if not in name, to be ruler of the British Isles by 1307? In fact, most of the ingredients for effecting such a transformation had long been to hand. First was the ideological justification. The Norman kings of England had inherited from their Anglo-Saxon predecessors a theoretical claim to the overlordship of the whole of Britain. It was a claim which could easily be reactivated and quite as easily provided with a supporting historical mythology, whenever the opportunity demanded.

Should kings have scruples about the morality of conquering Christian peoples, the papacy and its servants quickly came to the rescue of their consciences. Thus, in 1155, the pope sanctioned Henry II to assume control over Ireland in order 'to proclaim the truths of the Christian religion to a rude and ignorant people'. Over a century later, the Archbishop of Canterbury likewise provided Edward I with all the ecclesiastical justification he needed for his final campaign against the Welsh. If there remained any shadow of doubt about the propriety of English actions and motives, it was quickly dispelled by recalling that the Welsh and the Irish (and in some degree the Scots) were classified as 'barbarians' who were crying out to be civilized, especially in respect of their social practices and legal customs. The English self-evidently were to be the agents of civilization.

Ideological justifications apart, there were more practical reasons why the English should acquire domination of the British Isles in the twelfth and thirteenth centuries. England was ruled by an aggressive and acquisitive military aristocracy which responded to the calls of adventure, plunder and power wherever they presented themselves. Wales, Scotland and Ireland provided geographically convenient, if not necessarily the most appealing, targets for their restless energy and greed. Their greatly superior military technology — in particular the deployment of highly skilled, mounted soldiers and the building of mottes and ringworks to convert military victory into sustained domination — gave them over-whelming advantages, especially in their initial campaigns. Their enter-prises were supported, directly or indirectly, by the most powerful monarchy in north-western Europe. This monarchy commanded resources in men, supplies and cash with which the King of Scotland, let alone the petty rulers of multiple Welsh and Irish principalities and kingdoms, could not begin to compete. In the wake of the aristocratic warbands came peasant settlers hungry for good land as well as burgesses and merchants anxious to conquer new markets; they provided the essential manpower which could convert military conquest into permanent settle-ment — be they Flemings in Pembroke and Clydesdale or English settlers in Brecon, Lothian and Leinster. English domination of the British Isles was not merely a matter of political power and brute military force; it was also underpinned and accompanied by economic, commercial, cultural and religious dominance.

The story of Anglo-Norman and English expansion into Wales, Scotland and Ireland comes, therefore, as no surprise. It is an aspect of a broader story of aristocratic expansion and peasant colonization which characterizes the history of so many parts of Europe from the eleventh to the thirteenth centuries. Indeed, what is more surprising, given their apparently effortless superiority, is why the Anglo-Normans took so long to assert their domination of the British Isles. In truth, they had no grand plan to convert their theoretical claim to the overlordship of Britain into practice or to conquer 'Wales', 'Ireland' or 'Scotland' as such. Continental ambitions were nearer the hearts of most of them and, even within England itself, their energies were often diverted to their own domestic quarrels. In other words, domination of the outer reaches of the British Isles was not necessarily high on their agenda. Rather English power was extended within the British Isles as invitations were issued (by native rulers), opportunities seized and challenges met. There was little that was co-ordinated about what happened.

The faltering and long-drawn-out story of the 'conquest' of Wales bears out this claim. In many ways, Wales was an obvious and easy target for the Anglo-Normans. Its occasional military threat to western England, especially in the years immediately before and after 1066, provided ample justification for conquest; its attractive coastal lowlands and river valleys in the south had immediate appeal for acquisitive barons and land-hungry settlers; while its political fragility, fragmented as it was into small warring polities, afforded it little prospect of resisting the Anglo-Norman war machine. Conquest looked inevitable and easy. By the 1090s, the Anglo-Normans had established footholds in Anglesey and Pembroke, in the far north-west and south-west respectively. A generation later, the imminent demise of any semblance of Welsh independence could be confidently predicted: most of the rich lands of the south were controlled from Anglo-Norman castles, boroughs and priories; major settlements of English and Flemish immigrants had been established especially in Gwent, Glamorgan, Gower and Pembroke; meanwhile in the rest of the country native princelings could only cling on to the remaining vestiges of their power by acknowledging their client status.

Yet it was to be over a century and a half before the conquest of Wales was finally effected. This suggests that there was, after all, no great urgency about the process of domination. Apart from the lowlands of the south, Wales was not particularly attractive or rewarding to the Anglo-Normans, while much of its terrain was ill-suited to their military talents. For much of upland Wales a loose overlordship satisfied the needs of the English king well enough: Welsh princelings acknowledged his superiority, paid him occasional tributes, visited his court and sometimes accompanied him on his military expeditions. If they forgot their deferential status, they could quickly and easily be brought to heel by a swift and efficient military expedition, as happened in the years 1157, 1163, 1211 and 1241. If this was domination, it was domination on a very loose rein.

It was in the second half of the thirteenth century, and with quite dramatic suddenness, that this rein was violently tightened. By then the king and barons of England had come to terms with the loss of their lands in northern France; possibly Wales may thereby have acquired a higher place on their agenda. The king's perception of the nature of his overlordship in Wales certainly changed during these years, from that of an easy-going and relatively undemanding superiority to a more legally precise and judicially demanding suzerainty. Within Wales itself, the growth in the pretensions and power of the Prince of Gwynedd and his claim to the leadership of all the native Welsh posed a threat which the English magnates in Wales could not counter and which the King of England could not afford to ignore. So it was that what had been for almost two centuries a piecemeal and rather desultory process of English baronial penetration into Wales was converted into a direct confrontation between the King of England and the native Prince of Wales, between the English and the Welsh.

It was a fight to the finish. It was also a fight whose outcome was never in doubt; in truth, it was no contest. In two devastating campaigns in 1276–7 and 1282–3, Edward I demolished any surviving flicker of Welsh independence in what he himself declared to be 'a full and complete conquest'. The native dynasties were either extirpated or largely dispossessed; the north and west of the country was shired; a great statute introduced the laws and practices of England to the newly conquered districts; English-type administration, ultimately answerable to Westminster, was introduced with bases at Carmarthen and Caernarfon; and a magnificent group of castles proclaimed majestically the finality of the conquest. English domination was complete: 'the land of Wales with its inhabitants', so the Statute of Wales of 1284 triumphantly announced, had been 'annexed and united to the Crown of the realm of England'.

The story of English domination and conquest in Ireland has parallels with that of Wales; but the time-scale was different and so was the

12 *Observed by their parents and grandparents and, in the upper register, by the patron saints of the Welf and Angevin dynasties, Henry the Lion and Matilda of Anjou receive crowns from heaven.*

13 Château-Gaillard. Its fall in March 1204 was the prelude to the final Plantagenet collapse in Normandy.

14 King John out hunting (from a fourteenth-century manuscript). His ability to sustain energy for the chase of battle was more questionable.

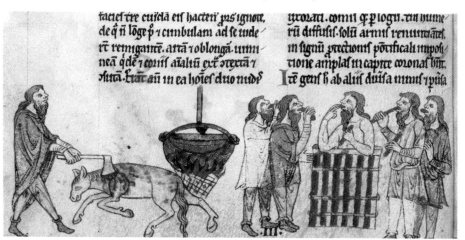

15 Henry III and his Queen return to England from France, 1260. An illustration from Jean de Wavrin's Chroniques d'Angleterre.

16 The English frequently represented the Welsh and the Irish as barbarians, desperately in need of being civilized. This illustration, from Gerald of Wales's Topography of Ireland, *shows a newly installed Irish king eating boiled horse-meat in a bath surrounded by some of his followers.*

17 Fifteenth-century portrait of John of Gaunt, now in the Chapel of All Souls College, Oxford, entitling him 'King of Spain'.

Alexander Rey Scotore

lewellin princeps wallie

PARLIAMENT

of EDWARD I.

18 This sixteenth-century illustration shows one of the great might-have-beens of British history: Edward I, flanked by the King of Scotland (right) and the Prince of Wales (left) as subordinate rulers in a session of Parliament. In the event it was by military power, not parliamentary control, that Edward I lived to become sole ruler of Great Britain.

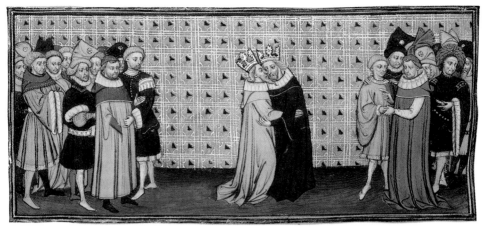

19 Edward III pays homage for Gascony to Philip VI of France; from the fourteenth-century Chroniques de France.

20 The murder of John the Fearless at Montereau, September 1419 — an act which drove Burgundy into the arms of Henry V.

21 Fouquet's portrait of the Dauphin, later Charles VII (1422–61).

*22 Caister Castle, built by Sir John Fastolf between 1443 and 1453
from profits made during his service in the French war under Henry V
and John, Duke of Bedford.*

outcome. For the first century after the Norman conquest of England, the Anglo-Normans showed little more than a fitful interest in Ireland; it was too marginal to the natural centre of gravity of their interests and ambitions. It was only by invitation from an ousted Irish ruler in the 1160s that adventurers from England and Wales first invaded Ireland, possibly spurred on by the rapid decline of opportunities for adventure and quick profit in England and Wales. Henry II followed hard on the heels of these aristocratic adventurers and their entourages, invading Ireland in 1171–2. Yet in Ireland, as in Wales, there was no original intention of a cmplete English conquest. Initially, Henry II seems to have contemplated no more than an acknowledgement of his title to Ireland, a firm foothold for himself in the south and east of the country, a goodly stake for the Anglo-Norman aristocracy and a working accord with the native Irish kings. But conquests generate their own momentum, especially when they are fed by aristocratic ambition and native discord. So it was that in the seventy years from 1170 to 1240 about half of the surface area of Ireland was brought under more or less firm English control. The transformation that was effected in those years was remarkable: English control of much of south and eastern Ireland was underpinned by a large network of mottes and stone castles; English and Welsh settlers migrated in large numbers (by contemporary standards) into much of the best agricultural land, founding manors and boroughs and transforming agriculture and trade; a dependent, delegated administration was established in Dublin, patterned on and answerable to the English government at Westminster; much of the country was shired; English common law and its institutions were transported thither *en bloc* and, by the end of the century, Ireland was even imitating England in developing its own parliament. The completion of the domination of Ireland by the English — a domination which was economic and ecclesiastical as well as military and governmental — seemed to be only a matter of time, and a very short time at that.

The time-scale and forms of English domination of Wales and Ireland were markedly different. But, by the 1250s, the end results in both countries seemed broadly similar: firm control by the English crown and a section of its aristocracy (albeit often absentee); extensive if uneven settlement by an immigrant English population, proud of its separate status and privileges; the introduction of many of the institutions of English governance, including ultimate judicial and financial control from Westminster; and the growing integration of the lowland and accessible parts of both countries into an England-dominated commercial orbit and economic lifestyle. Both Wales and Ireland had many of the distinguishing features of colonies, or annexes, of England; the same could not be said of Scotland.

Wales and Ireland, prior to the coming of the Anglo-Normans, were collections of small, warring and fissile principalities. Scotland, on the other hand, was at least in theory and pretension a unitary kingdom under a single king. Theory and pretension were brought much closer into alignment with political and governmental realities in the twelfth and thirteenth centuries as the kings of Scotland extended their effective control over the whole country (finally securing the Western Isles from the King of Norway in 1266) and built an infrastructure of authority which, though considerably looser than that which underpinned the power of the King of England within his kingdom, made the kingdom of the Scots an effective and politically cohesive unit. By the thirteenth century, Scotland also had a thriving urban and commercial life, especially in the towns of the south and east, and thereby a level of prosperity and wealth which enabled it to forge a variety of links with Europe. Scotland was now, in the words of one of its leading medieval historians, 'among the recognized powers of middle rank within the family of west European states'.

Relations between England and Scotland were, therefore, essentially different from those between England on the one hand and Wales and Ireland on the other. They were relations between two unitary monarchies, two rapidly developing kingdoms and between two well-integrated political communities. In the two centuries prior to the 1290s, the relationship between the two parties were, for the most part, good and, on occasion, cordial. From the early twelfth century Anglo-Norman nobles (such as the Bruces and the Stewarts) were invited by the King of Scotland to come to settle in his kingdom; indeed they were enticed with gifts of vast estates. The contrast with Wales and Ireland was striking: there the Anglo-Normans had largely arrived as warriors and conquerors; in Scotland, they entered by royal invitation and were rapidly assimilated into the social and political fabric of the kingdom. Social, marital and territorial links were quickly established between the kings and nobles of England and their counterparts in Scotland, and in many spheres — culture, government, laws, coinage, trade and the settlement of peoples — there was an easy rapport and fruitful exchange between the two communities.

The King of England, of course, took it for granted that he was the superior partner in the relationship; but he rarely felt the need to spell out that superiority formally. Political tutelage (such as that enjoyed by William Rufus and Henry I over the sons of Malcolm Canmore) or an interventionist paternalism (such as that which Henry III exercised over the young Alexander III) generally achieved their purpose effectively enough, without resort to grand declarations about constitutional relationships. If a Scottish king occasionally forgot that he was essentially a junior partner and should, therefore, not entertain pretensions beyond his status and power, he could quickly be brought to his senses by an English expedition (as in 1072) or a threat of one (as in 1209). Of all the Scottish kings, it was William the Lion who was taught the most brutal lesson about the realities of English superiority: captured in 1174 while laying siege to Alnwick Castle, he was taken as a prisoner to Normandy, compelled to do homage to the King of England for Scotland and his other lands and forced to accept English garrisons in three of his castles.

Fortunately, most Scottish kings did not have to undergo such humiliation in order to recognize that in their relations with England discretion was the better part of valour. Indeed, relations between the two kingdoms were particularly cordial in the period 1217–90 and were cemented by close marriage ties between the two dynasties. In 1290 it looked as if the two kingdoms were soon to be united, though their separate identity was to be formally safeguarded, by the marriage of the heir to the English crown with the heiress to the throne of Scotland. If so, the events of 1603 would have been anticipated and the two kingdoms conjoined under a single dynasty. But the plan was aborted by the death of the Scottish heiress in September 1290 and Edward I high-handedly used the occasion of the contested succession to the Scottish throne following her death to assert his direct and superior lordship over Scotland.

There has been much dispute as to whether Edward I, in the words of a contemporary chronicler, 'intended to subjugate Scotland just as he had subjugated Wales' or whether he responded legalistically and insensitively to events and opportunities as they arose. Be that as it may, the result of his actions on Anglo-Scottish relations was dramatic and permanent: an easy coexistence was converted in a few years into outright confrontation; an undeclared senior partnership was replaced by conquest and direct rule. Edward had not bargained with the resilience of the Scottish political community nor with its military skill and determination. Yet, once they had been deserted by their French allies, the

Scots did not have the power and resources to withstand the might of the English state. By 1305, Edward's control of Scotland, or at least of lowland Scotland, seemed well-nigh complete: almost all the major Scottish political leaders had submitted to him; the country had been demoted from the status of a kingdom to that of 'a land'; its kingship was in abeyance, if not abolished; the emblems of its independence had been carted off to England; an ordinance was issued at Westminster for the governance of Scotland placing the administration of the country under the control of three English officials directly answerable to the King of England.

By the autumn of 1305, English domination of the British Isles seemed at last to be almost complete. Wales had been conquered and its subsequent revolts (in 1287 and 1294–5) against English rule comprehensively crushed; English power had been extended to the furthest parts of Ireland and the administration and laws (at least of the settler community there) closely patterned on those of England; while Scotland had eventually been bludgeoned into submission, with the prospect that henceforth it was to be treated as a political, legal and administrative annexe of England. The dream of a single monarchy of Britain and Ireland, so long cherished in political mythology, seemed at last about to be realized. Nor was this monarchy to be merely a military hegemony or a loose federation. England now seemed to be sufficiently mature and self-confident institutionally for a measure of administrative and legal uniformity to be imposed on the lands dependent on it. Complete political and governmental integration might not yet be feasible, but eventual control from, and answerability to, Westminster were now among the hallmarks of English domination. With this background of English control, it might not be amiss to think of an English empire of the British Isles.

In truth, such intimations proved to be premature. The greatest promise and the greatest achievement were certainly in Wales. After the revolt of 1294–5, the Welsh presented no serious threat to English domination for over a century. Their militarism was channelled, as was indeed substantially the case before 1284, into the service of English kings and magnates against Scotland and France. Many of the leaders of Welsh society learnt to work with the grain of English governance, often to their own financial advantage. In social customs, legal practices and economic outlook the Welsh, especially in the lowlands and in the higher social echelons, were drawn increasingly into an England-dominated orbit. Conquest, so it seemed, was being followed by assimilation. Yet appearances deceived. Welsh resentment of the overbearing and extortionate character of English rule and of the privileges of English settlers, when combined with Welsh aspirations for the restoration of native rule, eventually triggered a country-wide revolt led by Owain Glyn Dŵr, a direct descendant of two of the native princely dynasties, in 1400. The revolt ebbed after 1406; but it left deep psychological scars on the relationship between the English and the Welsh. It showed that the Welsh were not to be trusted and that they had not abandoned their dreams and aspirations. Conquered the country might be; but its people were far from being assimilated into the political fabric and loyalties of the kingdom of England.

In Ireland, the prospects were even more disturbing. In 1341, it was forecast despondently that 'the land of Ireland was on the point of separation from the lands of the king [of England]'. The comment was unduly alarmist; but it revealed how the mood of expansive confidence of a century earlier had been replaced by deep gloom. Nor is it difficult to understand why. The age of English territorial advance had given way to that of retreat; local Gaelic chiefs were resurgent in different parts of Ireland; in 1315–18 the Scots had established a strong foothold in Ulster and even seemed on the verge of capturing Dublin. External and internal threat was accompanied by, and promoted, profound political changes within the English community in Ireland itself. As its ties with England were diluted and as it was thrown back increasingly on its own resources, so it cultivated its own identity, alienated both from the native Irish (whom it despised) and from an apparently uncaring and high-handed English administration and its provincial agents. The King of England, for his part, rarely placed Ireland and its problems high on his agenda. A country which had once brought him a handsome surplus in men, money and supplies was now a drain on his resources; its aristocracy seemed frequently intent on accumulating power for itself and frustrating his plans; the periodic dispatch of a royal lieutenant (such as Lionel of Clarence in 1361–6) or even a royal expedition (as in 1394 and 1399) showed how intractable were the problems of Ireland. At best, Ireland could only be regarded as a half-conquered country. Its native community remained as alienated as ever from English rule. Indeed, the Statutes of Kilkenny (1366) even further confirmed the institutionalized separation between the native Irish — 'the wild Irish, our enemies' as they were often now disparagingly called — and the English settler community. Whatever compromises might be arranged at local level, the official mentality remained one of conquest and separation, not one of assimilation and unity.

If the story of English domination in Ireland was turning out to be one of faltering retreat, in Scotland it was one of utter failure. The prospect of an English supremacy, so enticingly close in 1302–5, proved in the event to be short-lived, only to be briefly glimpsed again in the 1330s. Instead, the Scots, under the leadership of Robert Bruce, gradually reclaimed military control of most of the country and never again surrendered it. For over two centuries after 1306, the English and the Scots were sworn enemies, their relationships punctuated by fierce raids and counter-raids. The disparity in size, wealth and resources between the two peoples was immense. The English inflicted massive military defeats on the Scots on several occasions (as in 1332–4 and 1402); they captured the King of Scotland twice (in 1346 and 1406); and on one occasion (in 1513) killed him in battle. Yet, in spite of such disasters and in spite also of some heavy diplomatic arm-twisting, the truth was that the political independence of Scotland was no longer negotiable. Indeed, the prolonged war with England helped to confirm and deepen the Scots' awareness of their nationhood. No more eloquent expression of the right of self-determination was uttered in the Middle Ages than that of the Declaration of Arbroath of 1320 and no writers so assiduously created and cultivated the legends of a historic national independence as those of Scotland in the later Middle Ages. Scotland, instead of being yoked to an English partnership or even assimilated into an English-dominated polity, was now more securely and defiantly a distinct nation and political unit than at any earlier stage in its history. Even the English, reluctant as they were in theory to concede the political independence of Scotland, had no option much of the time but to accept the reality of it.

The prospect of a single monarchy and a single political society embracing the whole of Britain and Ireland — a prospect which to some contemporary observers had appeared so enticingly close c.1300 — had not materialized. The reasons are manifold. England's military and economic superiority was, of course, not in doubt. But the kings of England never gave more than spasmodic attention to the conquest and control of the outer regions of the British Isles. From the eleventh to the fifteenth centuries, the retention and augmentation of their lands in

France was consistently a much more prominent item on their political agenda. Furthermore, success in the British Isles was related, especially from the 1290s, to the fortunes of Anglo-French relations on a much wider diplomatic and military stage. The Scots, in particular, recurrently used their 'auld alliance' with France (first concluded in 1295) to give an international dimension to their struggle against the English. Even in Wales, Owain Glyn Dŵr seized the opportunity of an alliance with the French king in order to embarrass the King of England and to give his vision of an independent Wales some prospect of success.

The English domination of Britain and Ireland had depended not only on the initiative of kings but also on the enterprise and drive of aristocrats and settlers. The endlessly acquisitive ambitions of the Anglo-Norman aristocracy had brought much of southern Wales and southern and eastern Ireland under its control by 1250; members of this same aristocracy had likewise strikingly strengthened the consolidating ambitions of the Scottish kings and transformed the configuration of power in Scotland in the twelfth and thirteenth centuries. Aristocratic domination had been crucially underpinned by foreign settlement, as alien peasants and burgesses poured in considerable numbers (by contemporary standards) into the newly established manors and towns in Wales, Ireland and Scotland. By the early fourteenth century, however, the momentum of this remarkable aristocratic and settler diaspora was visibly faltering. In Scotland, the door of opportunity was slammed shut in the wake of the wars of independence; in Wales and Ireland, there were now few opportunities for easy fortunes and quick returns; the dramatic collapse in the population from the mid-fourteenth century meant that the incentive and the need for new settlements had now disappeared. In Ireland, especially from the 1290s, two terms were used increasingly to diagnose the mentality of retreat — 'absenteeism' (referring to aristocrats who resided in England and thereby avoided their responsibility to sustain the English planatation in Ireland) and 'degeneracy' (referring to the tendency of the settler English, now largely cut off from England and no longer renewed by further waves of immigrants, to 'go native' in language, culture and outlook).

But the failure of the kings of England to realize the vision of a single Britain and Ireland under their control was also in good measure a failure of governmental control and of political imagination. Military domination and victory were ultimately no substitutes for recognizing and responding to the political sensitivities and aspirations of the peoples of Wales, Ireland and Scotland and working at imaginative political solutions which might integrate them into a political community governed by the King of England. Even in Wales, which was more comprehensively and irreversibly conquered than Ireland or Scotland ever were, the settlement imposed by Edward I, magnanimous and imaginative as it was in many respects, fell politically far short of a solution. Formally, Wales may have been united and annexed to the crown of England, but in reality it remained an uncoordinated amalgam of royal shires and private lordships; it was not part of the kingdom of England fiscally or judicially; it enjoyed no representation in Parliament. Its people were treated, or regarded themselves as being treated, as inferior citizens in their own country — a sure recipe for a mythology of exclusion and for a deep sense of political alienation. The situation was even more unsatisfactory in Ireland: the incompleteness and fragility of the conquest were increasingly epitomized in the distinction drawn between 'the land of peace' and 'the land of war'; the native Irish were excluded from the benefits and opportunities of English law; their leaders were likewise excluded from regular participation in the affairs of the political community of English Ireland; even the English community in Ireland felt itself increasingly estranged from and neglected by the government in England and its agents in Dublin; while the phrase regularly employed to describe the native Irish, 'the wild Irish, our enemies', showed that in official circles the categorization of contempt and distrust still dominated the outlook of the English. As for Scotland, its stolid and eventually successful resistance to the pretensions of the English to political overlordship (or more) created a chasm of distrust and hostility between the two countries which lasted for generations. The easy affability of Anglo-Scottish relations in the thirteenth century was replaced by a mentality in which the Scots regarded England as the 'auld inemie'.

The unity of the British Isles which had looked so promisingly close in 1300 remained as far away, if not indeed further, in 1500. It would remain for future English statesmen and soldiers to seek to solve the unresolved problems — be it by political, legal and administrative assimilation into the English state (as happened in Wales in 1536–43), by the renewal of a policy of conquest and settlement (as happened in Tudor Ireland) or by a dynastic yoking of two crowns, to be followed eventually by a political union (as happened in Scotland).

CHAPTER XII

THE ORIGINS OF THE HUNDRED YEARS WAR

J. R. Maddicott

A T GHENT ON 26 JANUARY 1340, Edward III assumed the title of King of France. Although Anglo-French conflict had been an intermittent feature of the western European scene since 1066, no such grand and presumptuous a challenge to French power had been made by any previous monarch. It was a challenge which was to lead to more than a century of sometimes sporadic but often intensive warfare, punctuated by battles which made English arms famous throughout Christendom. Before the war ended in 1453, with the expulsion of the English from all their French possessions save Calais, the victories of Sluys, Crécy, Poitiers and Agincourt had created an heroic tradition of military success which not even the final disasters of Henry VI's reign could entirely obliterate. At home, the war shaped the course of English affairs for most of the fourteenth and fifteenth centuries. Whether we look at the development of Parliament, the growth of the export trade in cloth, the rise of national taxation or the reputations of kings, we shall find that political and economic change often hinged on the progress of the war. In examining its causes, we are to a large extent uncovering the roots of English history in the later Middle Ages.

Like many other wars, medieval and modern, the Hundred Years War had its origins in a peace settlement. The Treaty of Paris, made by Henry III of England and Louis IX of France in 1259, brought to an end more than a century of Anglo-French conflict; but its unintended result was to inaugurate first an eighty-year period of sporadic disputes and then a war which would last intermittently for more than another century. The treaty's main provisions, ratifying as they did the status quo, had hardly made this outcome predictable. By their terms, Henry abandoned his claims to Normandy, Anjou, Maine, Touraine and Poitou, the former territories of his Angevin predecessors, which had been lost to the French during his father's reign and his own minority, and which Henry himself had sought to regain, spasmodically and with diminishing prospects of success, for some thirty years.

By setting his seal on the formal dissolution of the Angevin empire, he had removed a potential *casus belli* which had embarrassed his generally friendly relations with Louis. In doing so, however, he had created another. In exchange for Henry's renunciations, Louis allowed him to retain the one fragment of the old empire which he still held, the duchy of Aquitaine (or Gascony), but to do so only on new terms: Henry was to hold the duchy as a feudal vassal of the French king. When Louis's counsellors reproached him with apparently conceding even this much, Louis made a reply which was more perceptive than their criticisms: 'It seems to me,' he said, 'that I am making good use of what I have given him, for Henry was not my man, and now he has entered my homage.'

He meant that he had succeeded in imposing his own overlordship on Henry and on Henry's duchy. Until 1259, Gascony had been held by its English king-duke as an *allod*, an independent territory held of no feudal lord and effectively outside the realm of France. Henry's novel recognition of Louis's suzerainty brought a partial loss of that independence and an entrée to the duchy for the French crown. Feudal subjection of this sort was not a mere matter of juridical theory, but carried tangible obligations. In the case of the king-duke, it meant in the first place the obligation to perform liege homage — more binding than simple homage — to the French king. This ceremony, entailing as it did the vassal's kneeling before his lord, placing his hands in his, and promising allegiance for his lands, was both personally humiliating and politically restrictive, for it carried with it the duty to provide military service when called upon to do so. Since it had to be performed at every change of lord or vassal — so that Henry III, for example, was summoned to do homage in 1271 after Philip III had succeeded Louis IX—it came to be a recurrent reminder of a debilitating subordination. And since failure to perform homage might legitimately lead to the confiscation of the duchy, the reminder was one which the vassal could not afford to disregard.

The recognition of French overlordship limited the English rulers of Gascony in two particular prerogatives essential to their authority: the making of foreign policy and the doing of justice. After 1259, no English king could, as Duke of Aquitaine, risk an alliance with his overlord's enemies or potential enemies. Such an alliance would constitute an act of defiance which, like the refusal of homage, would justify the confiscation of the vassal's fief. When Alfonso X of Castile sought the help of his brother-in-law, Edward I, against possible French intervention in 1275, Edward had to turn him down, for to have complied would have been contrary to his obligations to his suzerain. When Peter III of Aragon asked for similar help against a threatened French invasion in 1282, he too was rejected, even though Edward was then negotiating a marriage between his daughter, Eleanor, and Peter's son. In a comparable way, Edward was hampered in his dealings with Flanders, whose relations with France were potentially hostile, and sometimes actually so, for much of his reign. Edward's feudal links with France meant that he had to negotiate secretly with Count Guy of Flanders in 1292–3 and to deny help to the Flemings against the French in 1303. Such restrictions could be very damaging to Edward's interests. The security of Gascony depended upon his friendly relations with the powers south of the Pyrenees, and the English wool trade, whose profits Edward could tap through the customs system, depended upon stable links with the Flemish market. But on this matter as on many others Edward's vassal status in Gascony compelled both dynastic and national interests to give way before his obligations to the French crown.

The king-duke's judicial subordination was a more routine matter than these occasional crises in foreign affairs, but for that reason perhaps more onerous. After 1259, judicial appeals from his Gascon subjects could properly be heard by the Paris Parlement: an obstacle to effective rule which entailed the removal of the appellant from the king-duke's power during the period of the appeal and the main-tenance of a legal staff in Paris to defend ducal rights. Social and political conditions in Gascony were especially favourable to litigation and the appeals which litigation produced. Boundaries and jurisdic-tions were ill-defined, nobles and towns more independent than their counterparts in England, and ducal ministers often highhanded in their behaviour and difficult to supervise. The disputes and appeals which flowed naturally from these sources were frequently augmented by others deliberately provoked by French officials loyal to Paris and to the Capetian monarchy. It was a further mark of the same sub-ordination that the king-duke was expected to publish French legisla-tion with Gascony. These were serious intrusions on his control of the duchy. In an age when the doing of justice was a main constituent of effective lordship, and the number of litigants who sought judge-ments in his court a measure of a lord's power, the King of France had acquired an ultimate judicial authority in Gascony which its duke could not rival.

During the forty years which followed the Treaty of Paris, the latent conflicts which it had concealed came increasingly into the open. A generation after the lawyer Bracton had written that the King of England was under no man, but only God and the law, it began to seem incongruous that one who was a king in his own country should do homage to another king for his fief. In France, too, developing concepts of sovereignty made such a relation appear progressively more archaic and unstable. It had already been established by the late twelfth century that the French king, unlike the English, could not do homage to another man. During the late thirteenth century, and with increasing vehemence under Philip IV (1285–1314), French legists began to claim that their king was 'emperor in his realm'.

In a world of political absolutes, the position of a dependent feudal sub-state such as Gascony came to seem increasingly anomalous. At the same time, Philip's aggressive exploitation of his sovereignty began to impinge on Edward's powers, even within his own kingdom. When, for example, Philip asked Edward to provide ships in 1304 from Sandwich and other south-coast ports for the French war against Flanders, he was staking a claim to military service well beyond that traditionally due from Gascony.

Edward I, for his part, did what he could both to mitigate and to modify his feudal connections with his French overlord. He tried to make peace between France, Castile and Aragon, in an attempt to resolve his own conflicting obligations towards his allies and his suzerain. He endeavoured to place all appeals from subordinate courts in the hands of his seneschal of Gascony, so as to impede their dispatch direct to Paris. Most important of all, he began from the 1290s to claim that Gascony was an *allod*, held in full sovereignty. Despite the treaty of 1259 and the treble performance of homage (in 1259, 1273 and 1286), his lawyers argued that the treaty had been nullified by the failure of the French to complete the territorial cessions which were among its provisions. Barely tenable though it was, the claim showed both the frustration of the English government at the continuance of the feudal link, and also a hesitant move towards notions of English sovereignty in Gascony which were to be pursued even more forcefully some years later under Edward III.

Behind the Crown's defence of Gascony lay considerations of honour, family interest and profit. An ancestral possession, the duchy could be used as an appanage for the heir to the throne. As prince, Edward I was given deputed rule over Aquitaine and his two successors dukedoms there by their respective fathers. The intention was to give them a training in government and, in the case of the two creations of 1306 and 1325, to shift the onus of homage from a crowned to an uncrowned head. Gascon revenues made a more material contribution to royal power. Estimated in 1324 at £13,000, mostly from the customs duties on the wine exports for which England was Gascony's chief customer, they were worth more than the Crown's estate in England. And at a time when warfare was placing an unprecedented strain on royal resources, Gascony also supplied manpower. Piers Gaveston, Edward II's favourite, was only one of a substantial number of Gascon mercenaries and minor nobility who sought their fortunes in England during the Scottish wars of the 1290s. No English king, therefore, could afford to risk a French conquest of Gascony, for too much was at stake. When Philip IV confiscated the duchy in 1294, after a naval battle in the Channel between a Norman fleet and another partly manned by Gascons from Bayonne, Edward retaliated vigorously if ineffectively. The ensuing Gascon war of 1294–7, costing some £400,000, was almost certainly his largest single expense in a singularly expensive decade.

The war of 1294, terminated by a truce in 1297 and a peace settlement in 1303, showed how easy it was for the French to find a feudal pretext to attack Gascony and how vulnerable the duchy was to such an attack. Given the inconveniences of the feudal relationship, the growing assertiveness of Capetian power, and the difficulty of standing against that power, it may seem surprising that no wider conflict grew out of the Gascon imbroglio before the 1330s. Yet, until that decade, the tensions arising from the English position in Gascony were contained and controlled.

The peace of 1303 restored the *status quo ante bellum*, with all its potential for conflict, by returning the duchy to Edward in exchange for homage. But, at the same time, it appeased national rivalries by arranging for the marriage of Philip IV's daughter, Isabella, to the young Prince Edward. This marriage, which was later to provide the basis for Edward III's claim to the French throne, temporarily bound together the two royal families and induced Philip IV to take a more conciliatory attitude towards the affairs of Gascony. Two great 'peace conferences', the Process of Montreuil from 1306 to 1311, and the Process of Périgueux in 1311, though they ended in deadlock and recriminations, at least showed that both sides were willing to negotiate. Both, too, had other interests, external and internal, which precluded a major war between them. Philip IV and his two sons, Louis X (1314–16) and Philip V (1316–22), were too heavily committed to the control of Flanders and, in the long term, to the crusade, to have sufficient resources for the conquest of Gascony. Philip IV, in addition, had to face opposition from his nobles, which culminated in the provincial leagues of 1314–15. Edward II, for his part, was intermittently engaged for most of his reign against both the Scots and his own barons. His concern for Gascony was shown by his issuing a major reforming ordinance for its government in 1323; but he could not afford to be provocative there.

At the end of his reign, however, this brittle peace broke down. In 1324, the building of a *bastide*, a fortified town, at Saint-Sardos in Gascony by the last Capetian king, Charles IV, provoked first English reprisals and then French countermeasures which culminated in the confiscation of the duchy. Behind this incident and the ensuing war lay other differences — Edward's deferment of homage to the new French king, a rising tide of appeals to the Paris Parlement, French intervention in the duchy in response to disorders there — which showed that the consequences of the Treaty of Paris had still to be reckoned with. The settlement of 1327 which ended the war marked a hardening of the French attitude towards the treaty's legacy. Not only did Edward III have to promise a payment of £60,000 for his inheritance of the duchy and a war indemnity of 50,000 marks for French losses, but the French retained a large part of Gascony itself until the indemnity had been paid. The territories of the Agenais and the Bazadais, in 1307 worth about £6,500 a year or nearly one-third of the then value of the duchy, were removed from English hands. When Philip VI came to the throne in 1328, the revenues of the entire duchy were sequestrated until Edward's performance of homage in the following year. Even after this, tensions hardly relaxed. An attack on Gascony was planned by the French and expected by the English in 1329–30; Philip VI sought support among the Gascon nobility; and a third 'peace conference', the Process of Agen, which sat from 1331 to 1334 to deal with claims for compensation and restitution arising from the war, broke up without agreement.

The aftermath of the Saint-Sardos war thus inaugurated a new and colder phase in Anglo-French relations which was a direct prelude to the

Hundred Years War. After the earlier war of 1294–7 Gascony had been restored to its English duke, as we have seen. Philip IV's objective was most probably the full exploitation of his rights of overlordship, rather than the permanent confiscation of the duchy. After the Saint-Sardos war, however, the duchy was restored only in part. The retention of the Agenais throughout the early 1330s and the concomitant military manoeuverings implied a more overtly expansionist French policy which had the absorption of Gascony into the French realm as its ultimate aim. But, even at this stage, war might yet have been deferred or avoided, had it not been for the introduction of a third force into the relations of the great powers. That force was Scotland.

Scotland and France were old allies. Formally linked by treaty in 1295, they had renewed their alliance in the Treaty of Corbeil of 1326, by which each promised military aid to the other against the King of England. This pact reflected the nervousness of both parties in the absence of any firm peace with their common enemy, for at that time both the Anglo-Scottish war and the recent Anglo-French conflict were checked only by truces and not by treaties. Arising from these short-term needs, the treaty came to have much larger consequences in the period following the renewal of English intervention in Scotland in 1332. In that year, the 'disinherited' English nobles, who had been excluded from their Scottish lands by the Anglo-Scottish Treaty of Northampton of 1328, won a great victory. They defeated the Scots in battle at Dupplin Moor and allowed Edward Balliol to displace David Bruce as King of Scotland. Edward's own intervention followed in 1333, leading to a second and greater defeat for the Scots at Halidon Hill and, in May 1334, to David Bruce's flight to France. There, Philip VI stood by his ally: he announced to an English embassy, then in Paris to negotiate on the Agenais question and other Gascon disputes, that there could be no peace unless Scotland was included.

This was a crucial step on the path to war. French recalcitrance over Gascony, confirmed by Philip VI's declaration, was now linked with the French defence of the Scottish cause, in a conflict which Edward could not honourably abandon yet which he was far from winning. Despite successive campaigns and prodigious expenditure in the years after Halidon Hill, Edward lacked both the men and the money to put down Scottish resistance. Philip's assertion of support for David Bruce not only threatened to stiffen that resistance but also to open England to foreign attack. As early as 1333, the French had been planning naval raids on

England; further schemes were afoot in 1335 and 1336 to send a large naval force either to Scotland or to England; and some troops may actually have reached Scotland. The clinching of the Franco-Scottish alliance in 1334 had thus brought with it, for the first time since John's reign, a serious danger of French invasion; all the more serious because it threatened a state whose resources were dangerously extended in both Scotland and Gascony.

Philip was not alone in attempting to make common cause with his enemy's enemies during these years. Edward himself was beginning to play the same game, seeking support among rulers hostile or potentially hostile to France, and offering encouragement to some of the many dissidents who declined to accept Valois kingship. It was a game which he was to play with spectacular success during the 1340s and 1350s, and, like Philip's support for the Scots, it already threatened to turn a limited and containable rivalry into a much larger conflagration. In 1335, some of the princes of the Low Countries, disturbed by Philip's growing influence in their area and attracted by Edward's burgeoning military reputation after Halidon Hill, offered their services to him in the Scottish war. At the same time, Edward was negotiating marriage alliances with the rulers of Austria and Castile, neither of them friendly to Valois pretensions, and was about to open negotiations with others in the Low Countries. But the most significant of the malcontents whom Edward attracted was undoubtedly Robert of Artois. Robert had long claimed the county of Artois, held from France, against his aunt, Matilda, who ruled there from 1302 until her death in 1330. Philip VI had refused to accept his claim, and when Matilda died Robert was accused of her murder. He had fled, first to Brabant, and then, in 1334, to England. Two years later, he was declared an enemy of the French kingdom. Edward's continuing support for the fugitive greatly embittered Anglo-French relations: it was an open breach of his feudal obligations, made more offensive by Robert's apparent advocacy of military measures against the French.

From 1331 to 1336, however, these gathering differences were held in check by a project perhaps even more central to Philip VI's ambitions than his pursuit of Edward: his plans for a crusade. A successful crusade for the recovery of the Holy Land would vindicate Philip's kingship by reasserting the long Capetian tradition of crusade leadership and by confirming the French king as the leading monarch of Christendom. If the crusade was an expression of Philip's piety, it was also an aspect of his secular and expansionist aspirations, bearing comparison with his intervention in Gascony, Scotland and the Low Countries. To promote it, he set up a committee to deal with crusading affairs, negotiated with the pope for the raising of funds, gathered warhorses, ships and supplies, and sought the support of his nobility.

These activities, and the end to which they were directed, made it impossible for Philip to act with vigorous singlemindedness against Edward III, for all his sabre-rattling over Gascony and Scotland. Not only did he lack the resources to mount more than one large enterprise, but Edward continued to pose, though with diminishing sincerity after 1333, as a potential crusading ally. In March 1336, however, these material and moral constraints were suddenly swept away. Pope Benedict XII, fearing misappropriation of crusading funds by the French, continuing divisions among the feuding states of the west and the resultant failure of the crusade, cancelled the expedition. Philip's transfer of his crusading fleet from the Mediterranean to the Channel a few months later is traditionally seen as the immediate preliminary to the outbreak of war; and rightly so. For the first time, he was free to throw the full weight of his resources against Edward, and a full-scale invasion of England became a probability.

If the position of the English crown in Gascony was the ultimate cause of the Hundred Years War, and if the Franco-Scottish alliance, the threat of a French invasion and Edward's support for Robert of Artois were among its short-term causes, then Edward's claim to the throne of France was the final step which precipitated conflict. It provided a way out of the impasse which seemed likely to thwart Edward's military and diplomatic plans in the mid-1330s; but it is hard to think that it did more than that or that the war was in origin the dynastic conflict which it was to become. The claim arose from the death of Charles IV, the last of Philip IV's sons, in 1328. There were two possible contenders for the throne now vacated by the Capetians: Philip of Valois, nephew of Philip IV, and Edward III, grandson of Philip through his mother, Isabella. If the claim could be transmitted through the female (and here there was little guidance in law or precedent), then Edward had the better right. Edward's case had been put forward in 1328, but it had not been pressed, and, as we have seen, Philip had succeeded. Edward had virtually no support in France (even his father-in-law, William of Hainault, favoured Philip), and as a boy of sixteen under the tutelage of his unpopular mother and her lover, Roger Mortimer, the puppet ruler of an uneasy kingdom, neither at home nor abroad did he appear as a credible alternative to Philip.

Philip's victory over the succession was driven home by a demand for homage. Edward reluctantly complied in two stages, performing simple homage for Gascony in 1329, and then in 1331 acknowledging the stronger bond of liege homage. Philip had driven Edward into this long retreat through pressure on Gascony, first confiscating all its revenues until homage had been done and consistently threatening the confiscation of the entire fief — the normal and legal remedy for a lord whose vassal denied homage — until Edward had recognized his full feudal obligations. These transactions must have emphasized the bargaining power which Philip's overlordship of Gascony placed in his hands. After 1331, Edward's claim to the throne hardly remained even latent, for it seemed to have been effectively disavowed by his liege homage. Philip had apparently used his feudal control over Gascony with some skill in order to obliterate any possible threat to his throne.

Soon, however, the relative positions of the two kings would be reversed, and Philip would find himself facing a rival who saw the occupation of the French throne as the best means to the defence of Gascony. During 1336 and 1337, all the issues which had embittered Anglo-French relations for the previous decade came to a head. The move of the French crusading fleet to the Channel was followed in the summer and autumn of 1336 by attacks on the Channel Islands and on English shipping off the Isle of Wight.

A further and expensive English campaign in Scotland had brought no substantial gains. A French descent on England and direct intervention on the side of the Scots seemed to be very close. Negotiations in Paris concerning Gascony, Scotland and the crusade had once again come to nothing. Papal efforts to make peace delayed war for a few months, but could not avert it. The Parliament of March 1337 gave its sanction to an expedition for the recovery of the Agenais. The final break came in May, when Philip VI declared Gascony confiscate, using as a pretext the support which his vassal, Edward III, had given to his enemy, Robert of Artois.

In the end, the feudal relationship created in 1259 was thus the lever which turned contention into war. Edward's response was to issue letters of defiance, so cutting the link with his feudal suzerain, and to address them to 'Philip of Valois, who calls himself king of France'. This was both a denial of Edward's homage and, at the same time, an implicit claim to the French throne (though it was not until October that the claim was formally made). It was easy enough for his lawyers to argue later that his earlier acts of homage were invalid, since they had been performed without Edward's free consent and during his minority. No longer the rebellious vassal, Edward had cut through the tangle of feudal constraints which had enmeshed English relations with France for nearly eighty years.

War came in 1337 because of Edward's need to defend Gascony and his own country from foreign invasion. His claim to the French throne was a riposte both to the increasingly uncompromising and aggressive use of French power during the previous decade and to the related difficulties brought by his own aggression in Scotland. More provocative and less cautious than his grandfather Edward I, his support for Robert of Artois showed that he was not prepared to see his choice of allies shackled by feudal limitations. Yet it is doubtful if Edward himself saw the opening of war as a mere defensive reaction to threatening circumstances; for him it was a response to opportunity as well as to danger. He was, as the author of the *Scalacronica* had said, 'eager for arms and glory'. His victories in Scotland, however disappointing their aftermath, had shown him how greatly a king's reputation might be enhanced by success in battle. They were the talk of western Europe, and he seemed well placed to repeat them. He was practised in tournaments, and had deserved and won the support of his nobles. His bestowal of a dukedom on his eldest son and earldoms on six of his closest followers at the Parliament of March 1337 had been a token of his partnership with his great men.

To both king and magnates, the impending conflict promised chivalric enterprise, adventure, fame and riches. The world was all before them; and it was in this spirit that they went to war.

CHAPTER XIII

HENRY V AND THE DUAL MONARCHY

Nigel Saul

B Y 1420, AFTER LESS THAN THREE YEARS' CAMPAIGNING, Henry V had succeeded where his predecessors had failed. He had won the crown of France. Yet the Parliament held at Westminster in December that very year was the most critical his government had had to face. The Commons had begun to voice their concern at the implications for England of the Treaty of Troyes, signed seven months earlier, in which Henry was designated the heir of King Charles VI. They recalled the precedent afforded by Edward III's assumption of the French title in 1340 and petitioned for reaffirmation of the undertaking he had then given that his English subjects would never be put in subjection to him and his heirs as kings of France, a request with which Humphrey of Gloucester, the king's brother and lieutenant in England, was glad to comply.

This petition was one of several submitted in that Parliament which bore witness to the Commons' awareness of the constitutional implications not only of Henry's recognition as 'Heir of France' but also of his lengthy periods of absence abroad. Henry had been away since 1417. The Commons were anxious for him to return, but at the same time feared the possibility of a dissolution when he did. To allay this legitimate anxiety, it was therefore ordained that neither this Parliament nor any summoned in future by a guardian or regent should be dissolved by the arrival of the king in England during its proceedings. As it happened, Henry's homeward progress took somewhat longer than expected, and when it was rumoured that parliamentary petitions might be sent abroad to be dealt with by the king at his leisure, the Commons immediately demanded that all such petitions be answered within the realm and before the king returned home. This time, however, they had overreached themselves: the request was politely refused.

The constitutional vigilance of the Commons' was matched by a corresponding prudence with money. Hitherto, they had responded nothing if not generously to their monarch's appeals for financial support, but after the Treaty of Troyes their attitude changed. In legal terms, the war for the crown of France was over. The dauphin was disinherited and Henry recognized as Charles VI's heir. If the dauphin chose to keep up the struggle, that was of no concern to the English Parliament. The war between two nations had given way to one between the King of France and his rebellious subjects, in which the people of England had no part to play. Henry accepted the logic of this argument. He sought no taxation in the Parliament of December 1420, and 1421 was the first year of the reign in which none was collected.

Parliament, in fact, was doing no more than take at face value Henry's own formulation of his aims. He had always said that in claiming the crown of France he was seeking merely to recover his rights. He presented himself not as a conqueror but as a legitimate heir. To that extent he was following the example of his ancestor William of Normandy who, three and a half centuries before, had presented his case in exactly similar terms. He came, he said, not as foreign conqueror, but as the designated successor of Edward the Confessor; it was he and not the usurper Harold who was the legitimate heir. And the problem that confronted William after Hastings was the problem that was to confront Henry after Troyes: the reluctance of the defeated people to accept his rule. William was driven by successive native rebellions to dispense with the notion of continuity and rely ever more on the support of his Norman lieutenants. In theory he might be the legitimate claimant; but in practice he was the ruler of an occupied country. Likewise, in theory Henry might be the 'Heir of France'; but in practice the dauphin was still an alternative source of authority. Until he was eliminated, the new regime could not feel safe. Henry might hope that, given time, more of the feudal princes of France might be tempted to become parties to the Treaty of Troyes: the Duke of Brittany, perhaps, or the Count of Foix. But, on the other hand, he had no assurance that they would. They might be no less tempted to join forces with the dauphin to expel the English altogether.

Henry's design, moreover, contained another flaw. How was he to reconcile the promise given at Troyes to preserve the integrity of the French monarchy with the commitment he had given earlier at Rouen to guarantee the autonomy of Normandy? In 1418, when he had given that commitment, he could have had little idea that within two years he would be assuming responsibility for the affairs of the monarchy as a whole. Quite the contrary; at that time, as when he had set sail from Southampton in August 1417, the reconquest of the duchy probably represented the limit of his ambitions—a kind of Norman Conquest in reverse. But the murder of the Duke of Burgundy by the Dauphinists in September 1419 completely transformed the political situation. It drove the warring French factions further apart than ever. The Burgundians turned to the English as the lesser of the two evils and the alliance that was forged between them placed the crown within King Henry's grasp. Charles VI, old and feeble by now, was allowed to remain king for his lifetime; but on his death Henry was to succeed in all his dominions. Henry was to rule all the kingdom, not just a part of it; so, on his succession, Normandy was to revert to its status as a dependency of the crown of France. The greater cause of winning the crown had led him to forget, if not to ignore, a commitment, however vague, that he had given a year before. For let there be no mistake: preservation in full of the rights of the crown of France ran clean counter to the local particularism he had been appearing to encourage when dismemberment of those rights had been his aim.

Henry V, therefore, was no less opportunistic than Edward III had been three-quarters of a century before. Edward, having once staked his claim to the crown of France, had been willing in practice to raise or lower his demands in accordance with the fortunes of war. Henry, having renewed the claim, showed himself willing at first to settle for what his great-grandfather had been given, but then raised his demands to keep pace with the progress of his conquests. A bid for the crown itself might raise some problems — notably with his Norman subjects and, as we have seen, with the English parliamentary Commons — but it would solve far more; above all, it would circumvent the old and fruitless argument about the terms on which the King of England was to hold Gascony from the French king by making the Duke of Gascony himself the King of France. It offered the prospect of a bold and conclusive settlement of the centuries'-old antagonisms between the English and French monarchies.

In Henry's opinion a bid for the crown represented not the conquest of France by England but the creation of a dual monarchy in which each kingdom was to be ruled according to its own laws and customs. Henry's claim was a personal one: he was fighting to recover what he regarded as his legitimate inheritance; but, in the process of so doing, he was seeking to end the divisions between the two kingdoms and to unite the princes of Europe in a crusade for the recovery of the Holy Land.

These were large aims, but if any man stood a chance of achieving them it was Henry. He was not only a supremely gifted man, but also an extraordinarily energetic one, with a capacity to inspire others to work with equal single-mindedness in his cause. It is possible, just possible, that he could have brought the dual monarchy to fulfilment. But he was robbed of the chance to do so by his premature death in August 1422, two months before that of his father-in-law. It was his nine-month-old son, Henry VI, who was to succeed to the two crowns. Despite the loss of Henry's leadership, however, the English position proved remarkably durable. The military advance continued. Maine was subdued after the victory at Verneuil in 1424; and the idea of making the war self-financing began to approach reality. No more taxes were asked of the English Parliament until 1429, and then only for the special occasion of the expedition to crown Henry VI King of France in Paris. Success, Henry's heirs must have hoped, would breed success. The stronger the English position looked, the greater the chance of the French accepting it.

But whom did they mean by 'the French'? Henry's insistence on the recovery of 'his rights' conveniently ignored the question of the identity of the people whom he sought to rule. Despite the centralizing tendencies of successive Capetian monarchs, late-medieval France remained very much a country of provinces, of local particularism. Indeed, so far from swamping aspirations to separatism, the Capetians had the contrary effect of encouraging the feudal princes to form autonomous administrations within their own domains. Some of these princes, like the Duke of Brittany, capitalized on long-established feelings of regional identity. Some, indeed, went further, and sought by means of propaganda to make this identity a source of political strength. The Capetians themselves, it has long been recognized, used propaganda to promote loyalty to their own dynasty. On the principle that what was good for the goose was good for the gander, the princes did the same. Thus the Duke of Brittany's lawyers argued that *'le pais de Bretaigne est un pais distinct et separe dautres.'* And, for the benefit of those impressed more by visual images than by legal jargon, the ducal coronation service and other occasions for ceremonial display, like the chapters of the Order of the Ermine, provided a symbolic and heraldic representation of ducal authority. Brittany, it might be argued, was exceptional. It lay in a far corner of France and retained its own ruler throughout this period. But its eastern neighbour, Normandy, though much nearer to Paris, and though absorbed into the kingdom in 1204, was no less conscious of its own individuality. In the movement of protest which followed the death of Philip IV in 1314, it secured the one effective provincial charter that was granted at that time, the *charte aux Normands*. Small wonder, then, that in 1418 Henry V paid more than token respect to the duchy's desire for autonomy.

But the regional particularism that suited Henry as an opponent of the Valois monarchy undermined his authority as 'Heir of France'. To rule effectively, he needed the support of the princes and regional nobility; and if they were reluctant to give it to a king of the house of Valois, they might have been even more reluctant to give it to one of the house of Lancaster. Yet Henry's position, at least in the immediate aftermath of the Duke of Burgundy's murder, was by no means as hopeless as it appeared.

Some Frenchmen at least were prepared to regard him not so much as an enemy as an ally of the Burgundians, and the invasion he had launched not as a struggle between the English and the French but as an episode in a war between two rival French factions, Burgundian and Armagnac. In which case, support for the English did not automatically mean betrayal of France. The murder of the Duke of Burgundy at Montereau made it possible, indeed, to portray the war in personal rather than nationalistic terms. The dauphin could be stigmatized as a murderer. King Henry was the legitimate heir, and those who opposed him were traitors.

In the following decade, when the tide of fortune turned against the English, life became easier for those with troubled consciences. In 1422 Henry V died, leaving a nine month-old child, Henry VI, as his heir. And seven years later, in 1429, Joan of Arc arrived on the scene and became, as one historian has put it, both the symptom and the agent of the revival in French national sentiment. In July 1429, after breaking the English siege of Orléans, Joan escorted the dauphin to Rheims, where he was crowned in the cathedral. The dauphin — Charles VII — was now a legitimate monarch, and it became more difficult for the princes to deny him obedience. The Duke of Burgundy, for one, had to reconsider his position, and at the Congress of Arras in 1435 he abandoned the English alliance and renewed homage to his Valois cousin. In so far, therefore, as the Hundred Years War was a contest between the king and the princes of France, it was resolved in the end to the satisfaction of the king. He emerged from this century of strife with his hold over his mightier subjects greatly strengthened.

CHRONOLOGY

1415 Battle of Agincourt (25 October)
1417 English invasion of Normandy
1419 Assassination of John, Duke of Burgundy, by partisans of
     the dauphin at Montereau (10 September)
1420 Treaty of Troyes (21 May)
1422 Death of Henry V (31 August)
     Death of Charles VI (21 October)
1424 English victory of Verneuil
1429 Joan of Arc relieves Orléans (8 May)
     Coronation of the dauphin as Charles VII
1431 Joan burned by the English at Rouen (30 May)
1435 Treaty of Arras ends the Anglo-Burgundian alliance
1437 Charles VII enters Paris
1450 Surrender of the English in Normandy
1451 First reconquest of Gascony by Charles VII
1452 Gascon revolt against French rule
1453 The final fall of Gascony (20 October)

He emerged, indeed, with his hold over all of his subjects greatly strengthened. He used the emergency as a justification for collecting taxes without consent, and with the resources thus given him fashioned a standing army in the direct pay of the Crown. From this time, the English and French monarchies can be seen to be heading in opposite directions. At the beginning of the war, the English king had had the edge over his adversary in the ability to mobilize his nation's resources. Through Parliament, he was able to appeal not just to his immediate tenants but to all of his subjects to lend him financial support in a time of national need; and through their representatives in the Commons they usually responded generously. But, with time, the Commons came to learn how they could use the power of the pursestrings to demand changes in the internal governance of the realm and a measure of public accountability in the way their money was spent. The experience of the Hundred Years War therefore strengthened them *vis-à-vis* the Crown and encouraged them to develop a corporate identity as a political body representing the realm.

It was otherwise in France. Central assemblies had never been viewed with much favour by either the king or his subjects. The people of Rouergue on one occasion went so far as to say that

> they did not want anything to do with a general assembly of the kingdom, of Languedoc or Languedoil, because they were not accustomed to be in assemblies with them; but the *pays* of Rouergue was accustomed to have an assembly of its own.

Provincial assemblies had far stronger roots in popular sentiment than central ones, and were of far greater use to the king as a means of raising money. But the process of securing consent from one assembly after another was a slow and cumbersome business, and the war effort was often impotent while it was being undertaken; so, when the crisis facing the Valois house reached its climax in the 1420s, Charles simply bypassed the whole consultative process and collected the money on his own authority. There was scarcely a flicker of resistance. People knew that it was the monarchy and not the estates that had delivered the country from the invader.

To the extent that the emergency occasioned by the war was to lead to the decay of representative institutions across the Channel, the English parliamentary Commons were therefore wise to be on their guard in December 1420. True, they had little reason to suspect Henry of all people of seeking to impose taxation without consent; but in acknowledging the possibility that a future ruler, less scrupulous in his observance of customary procedures, might be tempted to invoke French precedent in English political life, they were in fact paying him the highest possible compliment. They were admitting that his dream of a dual monarchy might come true. In the event, however, it did not. It was an idea conceived out of its time. It would have stood a better chance of succeeding in the twelfth century than in the fifteenth, for Henry was set on uniting Christendom at a time when it was fast disintegrating.

CHAPTER XIV

THE END AND AFTERMATH OF THE HUNDRED YEARS WAR

Malcolm Vale

THE CONTINENTAL POSSESSIONS of the English crown were all lost to the French between 1449 and 1453, with the sole exception of the town and March of Calais. On 19 August 1450, James Gresham wrote to his 'right especiall master', John Paston, telling him that 'this same Wednesseday was it told that Shirburgh [Cherbourg] is goon, and we have not now a foote of londe in Normandie, and men arn ferd that Calese [Calais] wole be beseged hastily.' The events which led to the rapid collapse of English forces in Normandy, Maine and the duchy of Guyenne (or Aquitaine) delivered a profound psychological shock to the Lancastrian government in England and a severe blow to those Englishmen who had invested their energies and fortunes in Lancastrian France. Normandy fell with comparative ease; Guyenne posed rather more difficult problems to the French, for it was England's longest-held continental inheritance. Calais, conquered and settled with Englishmen by Edward III in 1347, held out and only succumbed to French power in 1557. The reasons for this apparently anomalous survival of English continental dominion will be suggested later. But why did the Norman and Gascon possessions of the Lancastrians fall so quickly to the French, and what effects did their loss have on English politics, trade and society?

The Lancastrian regime, or dual monarchy, in France had been created by the Treaty of Troyes between Henry V and Charles VI in 1420. Its collapse can be traced to the diplomatic setbacks of the late 1430s and early 1440s. Although Joan of Arc (d. 1431) had certainly helped to have the Dauphin Charles crowned at Rheims as 'rightful' King of France in 1429, the first clear signs of French military and diplomatic recovery were visible only after 1435. The defection of Philip the Good, Duke of Burgundy, from the house of Lancaster to that of Valois in that year greatly assisted this development. Some English contemporaries such as the veteran soldier Sir John Fastolf believed that Philip the Good's 'treason' marked the beginning of the end for Lancastrian France. But his volte-face did not spell immediate disaster for English war aims: Humphrey, Duke of Gloucester, routed a Burgundian besieging force outside Calais in 1436, and in fact Philip the Good never contributed substantially to the Valois war effort against the English. His resources were increasingly absorbed by the suppression of Flemish revolts and by the expansion of the Burgundian dominions in the Netherlands. The economic relationship between England and Flanders, mediated through Calais, was too valuable to be thrown away; mercantile truces to protect the wool and cloth trades were established soon after 1437. Nevertheless, because the Lancastrian regime was so heavily dependent upon Burgundian support within France, this loss gradually undermined it. Paris fell to Charles VII's troops in 1436 and this event had immense symbolic importance. The Lancastrian regime in northern France became more and more confined to the duchy of Normandy, with Rouen, not Paris, as its capital. This position was tenable; but only as long as the English garrisons in occupied Normandy were properly paid, victualled and disciplined. Otherwise, they preyed upon the local French population and aroused deep popular animosity. English military organization in Normandy had, on the whole, been effective and was one of the most durable legacies of Henry V (d.1422) and his brother John, Duke of Bedford, Regent of France until his death in 1435. Lancastrian Normandy was a viable concern, as long as these conditions were fulfilled.

The first symptoms of breakdown in Normandy were apparent soon after 1435. The death of Bedford removed an able and respected governor. Peasant revolts broke out in parts of the duchy and the Lancastrian regime failed to deal with the problems of disorder and brigandage (which had been contained by Henry V and Bedford). Violent disputes among English commanders about the direction to be taken by the war effort also took their toll. During the early years (1422–8) of his minority, Henry VI's government in both England and Normandy was surprisingly solvent. But, by the 1430s, financial problems pressed hard upon available resources. The estimates of income and expenditure produced by Ralph, Lord Cromwell, when he was appointed Treasurer of England in 1433, revealed a chronic deficit in the public revenues of the English crown. This was not because England was in any sense a poor or 'underdeveloped' country in later medieval terms. The surviving cathedral, collegiate and parish churches, with their elaborate chantry chapels, and the well-appointed castles and manor houses of the nobility and gentry do not suggest an impoverished nation in the throes of bankruptcy. Foreign observers commented favourably upon the quantity of meat consumed by the lower orders, in contrast to the largely bread-based diet of their continental counterparts. In the 1470s, the lawyer Sir John Fortescue wrote of the greater material prosperity found among the English rural population. However, a protracted foreign war of conquest and occupation, in contrast with the raids and plundering expeditions of the fourteenth century, made unprecedented demands on English resources. Not since the later twelfth and early thirteenth centuries, when the Angevin kings of England were forced to defend their French lands against the incursions of Philip Augustus, had the revenues of the Crown been under such continuous strain.

Public finance had parted company with private wealth in fifteenth-century England. The consequences of this tendency contributed significantly to the deteriorating situation in Lancastrian France. Many Englishmen were much wealthier than their fathers and grandfathers had been, but the Crown's ability to tap that wealth was very limited. The English upper classes were relatively lightly taxed: the burden of the parliamentary subsidy fell upon the rural population of the rank of yeoman and below. This had been fixed in 1336 at a tenth and a fifteenth of the value of movable goods in town and countryside, but manor houses and their contents were exempt. The machinery whereby taxes were raised and collected was also complicated and cumbersome. War did not wait for parliamentary taxation to be voted, assessed and gathered. Nor was the machinery for levying the customs duties on wool, cloth, hides and other commodities conducive to the rapid and effective mobilization of capital. The customs were increasingly employed as securities upon which loans were raised and this tendency ultimately destroyed the financial credibility of the Lancastrian regime. Creditors found that their loans were assigned for repayment upon sources of revenue which had already been pledged to others and there is evidence of attempts by the government to force loans from reluctant subjects during the crises of the 1440s and 1450s. There was thus very little incentive to lend money to the Crown unless the Exchequer offered cripplingly high rates of interest. While individuals made their fortune in both town and country — witness the clothiers and woolmen of East

Anglia and the West Country — the Crown fell deeper and deeper into debt. The end of the house of Lancaster in 1461 was in some respects a form of foreclosure upon a dynasty which was in fact both financially and politically bankrupt.

The Lancastrian war effort and occupation in northern France had for some time been underwritten by a few great creditors, such as Cardinal Henry Beaufort. His death in 1447 removed one of the major financial props of the government. It became ever more difficult to harness English resources and channel them towards the French war. From March 1449 onwards, military defeat followed upon financial exhaustion. The truce negotiated by the Duke of Suffolk with the French at Tours in 1444 had offered a brief respite from hostilities. But it was broken when the Aragonese mercenary captain François de Suriennes, who was in English pay, captured the Breton frontier fortress of Fougères. Spurred on by a powerful Breton faction at his court, Charles VII resolved to take punitive action against this act of truce-breaking and reopened the war with the English on 31 July 1449. In the short space of fifteen months, all the conquests of Henry V and Bedford in Normandy fell to the French. Maine and Anjou had already been ceded to Charles VII by Suffolk in accordance with the terms of an agreement in 1445, whereby Henry VI married Charles's niece, Margaret of Anjou. A combination of effective siege-craft and well-deployed artillery, combined with ruse, bribery and a successful policy of incitement of the local population and negotiation with English garrisons, reduced the duchy of Normandy to obedience by August 1450. However, English captains and their companies did not give up without a fight; even in these dark days, Sir John Fastolf's secretary, William Worcester, proudly recorded the deeds of Osbern Mundford, Fulk Eton, Matthew Gough and Thomas Gower. But the majority of these beleaguered garrisons negotiated surrenders with the French and were in effect paid to go away. What had taken over seven years to achieve was destroyed in under eighteen months.

In the duchy of Guyenne, however, different conditions prevailed. When they were released from involvement in Normandy by 1451, the core of Charles VII's standing army (the companies of *ordonnance*) were deployed against Henry VI's most ancient surviving inheritance in south-west France. The seizure of the possessions of his chief creditor, Jacques Couer, the royal *argentier*, and substantial grants of taxation from the French provincial estates gave Charles VII the necessary financial base from which to launch the last campaigns of the Hundred Years War. Gascon resistance to the French, however, was much more spirited than that of the Normans. The duchy of Aquitaine had been inherited by the Lancastrians from their Plantagenet predecessors who had held it without interruption since 1152; conditions there were quite different from those in Henry VI's recently conquered duchy of Normandy. By August 1451, the French had succeeded in taking Bordeaux, Bayonne and the rest of the duchy. However, in October 1452, a Gascon resistance movement (centred upon Bordeaux and led by merchants, shipowners and mariners) joined forces with an English expeditionary force under John Talbot, Earl of Shrewsbury. They recovered part of the duchy in Henry VI's name, but this success proved short-lived. A dearth of reinforcements from England and defections by some members of the Gascon nobility gave the French the opportunity to invade the duchy once again during the spring and summer of 1453. The siege-guns of Charles VII's masters of the artillery — the Bureau brothers — were devastatingly effective against Anglo-Gascon strongholds, and the defeat and death of Talbot at Castillon, on 17 July 1453, sounded the death-knell of English Gascony. The city of Bordeaux held out for another three months after Castillon, but this last bastion of support for the Lancastrian cause was forced into surrender on 19 October 1453. The Bordelais and Bayonnais then paid the penalty for resistance to the sovereignty of Valois France.

The loss of the French possessions inevitably made a deep impression upon the English, as well as the Gascon, subjects of the Lancastrian monarchy. Firstly, the sheer loss of prestige suffered by the Crown should not be underestimated. Henry V's achievement lay in ruins. Throughout the diplomatic encounters of the 1430s and 1440s, Henry VI had never formally agreed to renounce his claim to the French throne; in 1453, that claim was almost impossible to sustain. French reconquest was now a *fait accompli*. Although campaigns were mounted in the hope of recovering territory to support the French title under Edward IV and Henry VIII, the cards were now heavily stacked against the English. Dissension, disorder and civil war at home did not provide a stable base from which to launch expeditions and mobilize military manpower for foreign campaigns. Secondly, many Englishmen found themselves dispossessed as a direct result of the débâcles in France between 1449 and 1453. In 1452, Henry VI's government received a petition from those Englishmen who had fought for, but lost, their possessions in Normandy and Maine. Writing in French, they told the king that they

> have lost in ... Normandy, into which they had withdrawn, in con
> sequence of the recent conquest ... by your said uncle of France [Charles
> VII] all that remained to them of their moveable goods, upon which
> depended the livelihood of themselves, their wives and children; and at
> present most of them are completely ruined and reduced to beggary, which
> is a sad matter, given the good and just right you have to the said county
> [of Maine] and duchy of Normandy.

They requested the king either to compensate them adequately (as had been promised) or to make more determined efforts to recover his French inheritance. Allowing for the normal exaggeration of all petitioners, there was considerable justification for their grievances. Men such as Sir William Oldhall, Sir Baldwin Fulford, Sir Hugh Willoughby, Matthew Gough, Richard Frogenhall and many others who had held lands and offices in Lancastrian France may not have been 'reduced to beggary' by their loss, but they suffered severe blows to their pride as well as to their material fortune. A number of them held and continued to hold lands and investments in England, however, and this tended to soften the blow. Sir William Harrington, for example, *bailli* of Caen from 1438 until his expulsion by the French in 1450, actually increased his English lands during his service in France. On his return, he was elected parliamentary member for Lancashire in 1450–1. His near-contemporary, Sir John Popham, held extensive lands and lordships in Normandy, but nevertheless served as member for Hampshire in the Parliaments of 1439–40, finally returning to England to be elected Speaker of the Commons in 1449. However, he excused himself from the office on grounds of old age and long service to the Crown in France. The separation between Lancastrian England and Lancastrian France, where a kind of ascendant English gentry (on the Irish pattern) has been discerned, was never complete. Many men had been careful to keep a foot in both camps, for fear of losses, and it cannot be said that most English knights and esquires 'let Lancastrian France go to its fate ... because they had too little to lose there'. The most trenchant and vociferous supporters of the war effort, such as Sir John Fastolf, shire knight for Norfolk and Lord of Caister Castle, master of Bedford's household at Rouen, and Baron of Cilly-Guillaume, were not entirely exceptional among their class. Many English knightly and gentry families were represented in Lancastrian

France and had much to lose there. This had considerable bearing upon their subsequent involvement in English civil war.

What happened to the survivors? Some of those who formed the remnants of Talbot's army after its defeat at Castillon in 1453 found their way back to England by way of the sole remaining outpost of Lancastrian power abroad — the garrison at Calais. Others came back in the followings of the lords and captains whom they had served in France, but we have an incomplete picture of their subsequent careers. A tiny minority remained in Valois France: Sir John Merbury, for instance, who had married a Frenchwoman, took the oath of allegiance to the French and became a counsellor and chamberlain to Charles VII. The Welsh captain, John Edwards, surrendered La Roche-Guyon to them and also took the oath, for he too had a French wife. But the overwhelming majority of the dispossessed returned to England, some to serve Richard, Duke of York; others to remain in the Lancastrian camp. Those who had once fought the French together survived to fight each other at St Alban's, Barnet and Towton.

Other Englishmen, who held no landed or movable property in Lancastrian France, nevertheless had important mercantile and commercial connections with the former French possessions. The vintners, shipowners and mariners who traded in Gascon wine evidently felt the loss of Guyenne acutely. During the first half of the fifteenth century, about seventy-five per cent of the shipping which paid customs duties at the port of Bordeaux was owned and largely manned by Englishmen. A great vessel such as the *Trinity* of Dartmouth, with a tonnage of 400 tuns, a crew of eighty and a complement of nine guns, regularly made the crossing to Bordeaux in the annual convoy of about 120 ships which brought the Gascon vintage to England. The French seizures of Guyenne in 1451 and 1453 immediately broke the English monopoly over the wholesale, retail and carrying trade in Gascon wine. An export figure of 12,000 tuns had been reached between 1444 and 1449; it declined to between 2,000 and 4,000 tuns during the 1450s and 1460s. Breton, Norman, Spanish and Hanseatic ships filled the gap left by the ending of the English monopoly. A surge of mercantile protectionism afflicted English ports and traders. In 1467, for example, the authorities at Bristol refused to unload Gascon wine from Spanish ships and some of the origins of the later Tudor Navigation Acts may be seen in such measures. The Gascons were no longer subjects of the English crown, nor did English shipowners and traders any longer enjoy a privileged position in the trade with Bordeaux. There was good cause for complaint among the sea-faring communities of western and southern England. It was no coincidence that the search for new markets and sources of supply — Iceland, the Baltic, Spain and the Americas — was led by the mariners of the western ports, well schooled in ocean-going seamanship through their trade with south-west France.

It has been claimed that the collapse of English rule in France between 1449 and 1453 led to a distinct shift in English preoccupations and ambitions abroad. The so-called 'continentalist' policy of the fourteenth and fifteenth centuries, based upon claims to rights and territories overseas, was gradually to give way to the insularity of the Tudors, which rested upon English sea power. The Channel and Western Approaches were to become parts of a 'moat defensive' rather than highways of commerce and military activity. But this contrast can be overdrawn. A contemporary tract known as the *Libel of English Policy* (c.1436) asserted the importance of England's 'moat' and the necessity of 'safely keeping the narrow seas'. It was particularly important to provide some degree of security for the narrowest sea of all — the English Channel, especially between the southern coastal ports and Calais. With the loss of Harfleur, Cherbourg, Bordeaux and Bayonne, English bridge-heads and points of entry into France were drastically reduced at a stroke. Apart from its essential role as an entrepôt for English commerce with the mainland of north-west Europe, Calais possessed a wider significance. The establishment of a wool and cloth staple there, through which all English exports passed, led to the creation of a permanent colony of English residents whose connections lay with the Low Countries rather than with France. Their colleagues and kinsmen in England acted as intermediaries between England and the Continent. Families such as the Celys and the Donnes held administrative positions and maintained mercantile interests at Calais, while the lieutenancies exercised there by Warwick (the 'Kingmaker') and William, Lord Hastings, Chamberlain to Edward IV, also drew men towards the Low Countries in the service of these magnates.

This tendency was furthered by the renewal of the Anglo-Burgundian alliance which had disintegrated in 1435. The Yorkist monarchy of Edward IV was supported by the Burgundians and in 1468 the alliance of the two houses was cemented and formalized by the marriage of Edward's sister, Margaret of York, to Charles the Bold of Burgundy. With Burgundian power behind it, England's hold on Calais was strengthened.

Calais was the gateway to what are now termed the 'Burgundian Netherlands' — Flanders, Brabant, Hainault, Holland, Zeeland and Luxembourg — and much diplomatic and commercial traffic flowed through it from England to Bruges, Brussels and the other great towns of the Low Countries. The collapse of Charles's regime in 1477, when he was defeated and killed by a coalition of his enemies at Nancy, did not sever the connection with England because his successors — the Austrian and Spanish Habsburgs — saw England as a useful partner in their conflicts with France. The economic interests of their Netherlandish territories were, moreover, still partly dependent upon English markets and sources of supply. A slow reorientation of England's commercial and cultural relations with northern Europe took place, in which the loss and abandonment of French lands and titles gave way to closer and more productive relationships with the Low Countries. William Caxton published books in Bruges before he set up his printing presses in London and the close contacts between the English company of the Staple at Calais and the citizens and nobles of the Netherlandish towns brought cultural as well as economic benefits to England. At the level of aristocratic and courtly society Burgundian influences were also strong.

The renewed Burgundian alliance of Edward IV (1461–83) was thus productive of cultural, as well as political and economic developments. England's latent cultural isolationism, previously tempered by her relationship with France, was arrested. Burgundian and Netherlandish influences were transmitted through individuals such as Louis de Bruges, Lord of La Gruthuyse (d.1492), who was created Earl of Winchester by Edward IV in 1472. Louis de Bruges had harboured Edward in his house at Bruges during the king's exile in the Low Countries (1470–1) and was a lavish patron of the arts. Caxton drew books from his library for translation and publication. Louis de Bruges's inspiration may lie behind Edward's commissioning of a series of large, de luxe, illuminated manuscripts from the workshops of Bruges and Ghent. He may also have influenced the king's decision to rebuild the Garter chapel of St George at Windsor, modelling the royal pew upon the Gruthuyse oratory in the church of Our Lady at Bruges. Burgundian inspiration clearly lay behind Edward's revival of the Order of the Garter, in emulation of the Burgundian Golden Fleece. Unlike his father, Charles the Bold accepted the Garter and a conscious attempt to imitate Burgundian chivalry in jousts, tourneys and feasting characterized Edward IV's court. It was quite unlike that of Henry VI and Margaret of Anjou. Sir John II Paston wrote to his brother John in the spring of 1467, telling him:

> My hand was hurte at the Tourney at Eltham upon Wednesday last; I would that you had been there and seen it, for it was the goodliest sight that was sene in Inglande this forty yeares of so few men. There was upon the one side within, the Kinge, my Lorde Scales, myselfe, and Sellenger, and without, my Lord Chamberlyn [Hastings], Sir John Woodvyle, Sir Thomas Mountgomery and John Parre.

John II Paston and his brother were at Bruges for the wedding of Margaret of York and Charles the Bold in 1468 and John III described the Burgundian court in glowing terms: 'I herd never of non lyke to it save Kyng Artourys cort.' The emphasis placed by the Valois dukes of Burgundy upon their household as an instrument of power and patronage was paralleled in England by the creation of a king's 'affinity' (or body of nobles and gentlemen holding household offices) at the Yorkist court. In 1474, Olivier de La Marche, Charles the Bold's chamberlain, wrote his famous description of the Burgundian household at Edward IV's request. This tendency to adopt the practices of the court of Burgundy continued into the reigns of Henry VII and Henry VIII.

Besides the dominance achieved by Burgundian courtly culture in England at this time, other aspects of English artistic activity were greatly influenced by close contacts with the Low Countries. English royal and episcopal palaces, for instance, owed much to Netherlandish example and the building of Richmond Palace under Henry VII adopted many Flemish stylistic and domestic arrangements. The origins of the long gallery in English country houses of a later date is to be sought during this period, for galleries flanking courtyards or gardens had been a feature of Burgundian ducal palaces for some time. Flemish and Dutch vernacular architecture, with its brick construction, gables, vanes and ornamental motifs was to be as significant an influence upon English Renaissance architecture as anything produced in France or Italy.

Similar conclusions can be reached for the visual arts, literature and music. English glass- and panel-painting were influenced by Netherlandish styles and were sometimes produced by Flemish artists and craftsmen. At least two affluent Englishmen patronized Flemish painters: Edward Grimston, esquire, was portrayed by Petrus Christus in 1448, while Sir John Donne 'of Calais' commissioned a triptych from Hans Memling at

Bruges in about 1480. Both works now hang in the National Gallery, London. Secular literature was also subject to the influence of themes drawn from chivalric romances, many of which had been reworked in prose form at and for the court of Burgundy. Sir Thomas Malory drew his *Le Morte d'Arthur* from a 'Frensshe boke' of this kind and the adaptation (and transformation) of all kinds of literature that circulated in the courts and cities of France and the Low Countries again kept England within a cultural milieu which owed much to continental sources. As we have already seen, Caxton's list of translations into English of both secular and religious books reads rather like the contents of a Burgundian library. The early humanism of the Low Countries was, moreover, soon to be carried to England by John Colet and Thomas More, and Erasmus was to find some sympathy for his views there. The Burgundian Netherlands played an important part in the dissemination of Italian humanistic ideas to northern Europe, and this was to have implications for English cultural development.

Music had also played a central part in the flowering of the arts associated with the Burgundian lands in the Middle Ages. New developments in both vocal and instrumental music originated in the Netherlands and the expressive and elaborate part-writing for choirs which influenced other European countries, not least Italy, emerged from the cathedrals and parish churches of Cambrai, Lille and Bruges. Choral polyphony of this kind was a true *ars nova* (new art-form) and composers such as Guillaume Dufay, Gilles Binchois and Jean Ockeghem both influenced, and were influenced by, English musicians such as John Dunstable and Robert Morton. The English chapel royal thus entered the Tudor period fully conversant with the polyphonic styles of the Netherlands.

Influences such as these — some of them reciprocal — ensured that England did not become culturally isolated after the loss of her French possessions in the mid-fifteenth century. A strong vernacular literary culture certainly existed, as well as a robust patriotism which was exploited by the Tudors, but this did not lead to isolationism. The first major breach between England and the European continent — the loss of the remaining French dominions — certainly accelerated existing tendencies towards a sense of national identity which had developed during the Hundred Years War. But these were to some extent offset by closer links with the Low Countries and by a strengthening of relations with the Protestant German states and the Baltic lands. The second breach — the English Reformation — was to drive a wedge between England and Catholic France, Flanders and Spain which endured until the eighteenth century and beyond. It is sometimes argued that England's development was unique because the kingdom formed part of an island. There were none the less grounds for suggesting that, even after her continental power-base had disappeared, England formed an outpost of north-west Europe, linked by economic and cultural ties to the Atlantic seaboard of the Continent. It was not long before involvement in European wars once again brought English soldiers across the Channel. Although the Hundred Years War had effectively ended in 1453, English armies never entirely deserted the battlefields of Europe.

FURTHER READING

CHAPTER I
England and Europe: Problems and Possibilities

The Hereford World Map is discussed and illustrated in *Age of Chivalry: Art in Plantagenet England 1200–1400*, ed. J. Alexander and P. Binski (London, 1987). For links between England and the Continent before 1066 see J. M. Wallace-Hadrill, *Early Germanic Kingship in England and on the Continent* (Oxford, 1970), and W. Levison, *England and the Continent in the Eighth Century* (Oxford, 1946); and for the period after 1066 the essays by R. W. Southern in his *Medieval Humanism and Other Studies* (Oxford, 1970). Emergent English national identity is a theme of M. T. Clanchy, *England and its Rulers 1066–1272* (London, 1983).

CHAPTER II
England and the Continent in the Anglo-Saxon Period

P. Grierson, 'The Relations between England and Flanders before the Norman Conquest', *Transactions of the Royal Historical Society*, 4th series 23 (1941), reprinted in *Essays in Medieval History*, ed. R. W. Southern (London, 1968); F. Barlow, *The English Church 1000–1066* (London, 1966); D. Bullough, 'The Continental Background of the Reform', *Tenth-Century Studies*, ed. D. Parsons (London-Chichester, 1975); J. Campbell, 'England, France and Germany: Some Comparisons and Connexions', *Ethelred the Unready*, ed. D. Hill, BAR British Series 79 (Oxford, 1978); S. Keynes, 'The Æthelings in Normandy', *Anglo-Norman Studies* 13 (1991); M. K. Lawson, *Cnut: the Danes in England in the Early Eleventh Century* (London, 1993), P. Stafford, *Unification and Conquest: A Political and Social History of England in the Tenth and Eleventh Centuries* (London, 1989).

CHAPTER III
The Norman Conquest

The early history of Normandy is considered by D. Bates, *Normandy before 1066* (London, 1982). Useful general surveys of the Conquest and its effects are offered

by R. A. Brown, *The Normans and the Norman Conquest* (London, 1969) and
M. Chibnall, *Anglo-Norman England 1066–1166* (Oxford, 1986). The best
biography of William the Conqueror is D. Douglas, *William the Conqueror*
(London, 1964).

CHAPTER IV
The Norman World of Art

English Romanesque Art 1066–1200, Arts Council of Great Britain exhibition
catalogue (London, 1984); *The Golden Age of Anglo-Saxon Art*, British Museum
and British Library exhibition catalogue (London, 1984); G. Zarnecki, '1066 and
architectural sculpture', *Proceedings of the British Academy*, LII (1966).

CHAPTER V
The Monastic Revival

C. H. Lawrence, *Medieval Monasticism: Forms of Religious Life in Western
Europe in the Middle Ages*, 2nd edition (London, 1989); M. D. Knowles, *The
Monastic Order in England* (2nd edition, Cambridge, 1963); Colin Platt, *The
Abbeys and Priories of Medieval England* (London, 1984); R. W. Southern, *St.
Anselm and his Biographer* (Cambridge, 1963).

CHAPTER VI
The Angevin Empire

The only treatment of the Angevin empire as a whole is John Gillingham, *The
Angevin Empire* (London, 1984), which contains an up-to-date bibliography;
W. L. Warren, *Henry II* (London, 1973), is the best biography of its subject.
Differing views about the nature of the Angevin empire are expressed in the
following essay collections: John Le Patourel, *Feudal Empires: Norman and
Plantagenet* (London, 1985); C. Warren Hollister, *Monarchy, Magnates and
Institutions in the Anglo-Norman World* (London, 1985); J. C. Holt, *Magna
Carta and Medieval Government* (London, 1985).

CHAPTER VII
Germany and England 1066–1453

D. Abulafia, *Frederick II: A Medieval Emperor* (London, 1988); C. C. Bayley,
'The diplomatic preliminaries of the double election of 1257 in Germany', *English
Historical Review* 72, (1947); N. Denholm-Young, *Richard of Cornwall* (Oxford,
1947); P. Dollinger, *The German Hansa*, trans. D. S. Ault and S. H. Steinberg

(London and Basingstoke, 1970); F. R. H. du Boulay, *Germany in the later Middle Ages* (London, 1983); A. Haverkamp, *Medieval Germany 1056–1273*, trans. H. Braun and R. Mortimer (Oxford, 1988); K. Jordan, *Henry the Lion: A Biography*, trans. P. S. Falla (Oxford, 1986); K. J. Leyser, *Medieval Germany and its Neighbours 900–1250* (London, 1982); C. C. Mierow and R. Emery, *The Deeds of Frederick Barbarossa by Otto of Freising and his continuator, Rahewin*, Records of Civilization, Sources and Studies (New York, 1953); P. Munz, *Frederick Barbarossa: A study in medieval politics* (London, 1969); T. Reuter, 'John of Salisbury and the Germans', *The World of John of Salisbury*, Studies in Church History, Subsidia, vol. 3 (Oxford, 1984).

CHAPTER VIII
The Fall of the Angevin Empire

Still the only major work on the collapse of the Angevin empire, and wider in scope than its title suggests, is F. M. Powicke, *The Loss of Normandy* (Manchester, 1960). By far the liveliest biography of John is W. L. Warren, *King John* (London, 1961). On Philip Augustus see J. W. Baldwin, *The Government of Philip Augustus* (Berkeley, California, 1986). The case for the greater wealth of the Capetian kingdom has been powerfully put by J. C. Holt, 'The Loss of Normandy and Royal Finance', *War and Government in the Middle Ages*, ed. John Gillingham and J. C. Holt (London, 1984). For the opposing view see John Gillingham, *The Angevin Empire* (London, 1984).

CHAPTER IX
England and Gascony 1216–1337

Margaret Wade Labarge, *Gascony, England's First Colony 1204–1453* (London, 1980) tells a straightforward story but has now been largely superseded by Malcolm Vale, *The Angevin Legacy and the Hundred Years War* (Oxford, 1990); this is the most authoritative account of Anglo-Gascon relations to date. J. Le Patourel, *Feudal Empires: Norman and Plantagenet*, ed. M. Jones (London, 1984) is a collection of this most distinguished historian's seminal essays. G. P. Cuttino, *English Medieval Diplomacy* (Bloomington, Indiana, 1985) contains a useful summary of the terms of the Treaty of Paris, 1259. Most recent research is represented by articles including J. A. Kicklighter, 'French Jurisdictional Supremacy in Gascony; one aspect of the ducal government's response', *Journal of Medieval History* (1979), 127–134 and J. R. Studd, 'The Marriage of Henry of Almain and Constance of Béarn', *Thirteenth Century England iii*, ed. P. R. Coss and S. D. Lloyd (Woodbridge, 1991).

CHAPTER X
Before the Armada: Iberia and England in the Middle Ages

W. R. Childs, *Anglo-Castilian Trade in the Later Middle Ages* (Manchester, 1978); D. W. Lomax, 'The First English Pilgrims to Santiago de Compostela', *Studies in Medieval History presented to R. H. C. Davis*, ed. H. Mayr-Harting and R. I. Moore (London and Ronceverte, 1985); A. MacKay, *Spain in the Middle Ages* (London, 1977); Joanot Martorell and Martí Joan de Galba, *Tirant Lo Blanc*, trans. D. H. Rosenthal (London, 1984); J. F. O'Callaghan, *A History of Medieval Spain* (Ithaca, New York, 1975); A. H. de Oliveira Marques, *History of Portugal*, I (New York, 1972); P. E. Russell, *The English Intervention in Spain and Portugal in the Time of Edward III and Richard II* (Oxford, 1955).

CHAPTER XI
The Failure of the First British Empire? England's Relations with Ireland, Scotland and Wales 1066–1500

Much the best general review is now to be found in Robin Frame, *The Political Development of the British Isles 1100–1400* (Oxford, 1990). The assumptions and mentality of English expansion are considered in R. R. Davies, *Domination and Conquest: The Experience of Ireland, Scotland and Wales 1100–1300* (Cambridge, 1990). For the wider European context see Robert Bartlett, *The Making of Europe. Conquest, Colonization and Cultural Change* (London, 1993). The issues are best approached from the viewpoint of a particular country in the following books: for Ireland, R. Frame, *Colonial Ireland, 1169–1369* (Dublin, 1981) and J. F. Lydon, *The Lordship of Ireland in the Middle Ages* (Dublin, 1972); for Scotland, G. W. S. Barrow, *Kingship and Unity: Scotland 1100–1306* (London, 1981) and A. Grant, *Independence and Nationhood: Scotland 1306–1469* (London, 1984); and for Wales, R. R. Davies, *The Age of Conquest: Wales 1063–1415* (Oxford, 1991) and G. Williams, *Recovery, Reorientation and Reformation: Wales c.1415–1642* (Oxford, 1987).

CHAPTER XII
The Origins of the Hundred Years War

E. Perroy, *The Hundred Years War* (London 1959); *The Hundred Years War*, ed. K. Fowler ('Problems in Focus' Series, London 1971); M. W. Labarge, *Gascony: England's First Colony, 1204–1453* (London, 1980); K. Fowler, *The Age of Plantagenet and Valois* (London, 1967); J. P. Trabut-Cussac, *L'Administration Anglaise en Gascogne sous Henry III et Edouard I de 1254 à 1307* (Paris, 1972); F. M. Powicke, *The Thirteenth Century* (Oxford, 1953).

CHAPTER XIII
Henry V and the Dual Monarchy

E. F. Jacob, *Henry V and the Invasion of France* (London, 1947); C. T. Allmand, *Lancastrian Normandy* (Oxford, 1983); C. T. Allmand, *Henry V, 1415–1450: the History of a Medieval Occupation* (London, 1992).

CHAPTER XIV
The End and Aftermath of the Hundred Years War

The following books and articles will supply further information and ideas about this subject: C. T. Allmand, *Lancastrian Normandy, 1415–1450: The History of a Medieval Occupation* (Oxford, 1983); M. H. Keen, *England in the Later Middle Ages* (London, 1979) and his articles 'The End of the Hundred Years War. Lancastrian France and Lancastrian England', *England and her Neighbours, 1066–1453: Essays in Honour of Pierre Chaplais*, ed. M. Jones and M. Vale (London, 1989) and (with M. J. Daniel) 'English Diplomacy and the Sack of Fougères in 1449', *History*, LIX (1974); M. G. A. Vale, *English Gascony, 1399–1453* (Oxford, 1970) and 'The Last Years of English Gascony, 1451–1453', *TRHS*, 5th series, XIX (1969); K. B. McFarlane, *The Nobility of Later Medieval England* (Oxford, 1973) and *England in the Fifteenth Century*, ed. G. L. Harriss (London, 1981); G. L. Harriss, *Cardinal Beaufort* (Oxford, 1988); A. E. Curry, 'The First English Standing Army? Military Organisation in Lancastrian Normandy, 1420–1450', *Patronage, Pedigree and Power in Later Medieval England*, ed. C. D. Ross (Gloucester and Totowa, 1979); and R. Massey, 'The Land Settlement in Lancastrian Normandy', *Property and Politics: Essays in Later Medieval English History*, ed. A. J. Pollard (Gloucester, 1984). For Burgundy and Anglo-Burgundian relations see R. Vaughan, *Philip the Good: The Apogee of Burgundy* (London, 1970); C. A. J. Armstrong, *England, France and Burgundy in the Fifteenth Century* (London, 1983) and 'The Golden Age of Burgundy', *The Courts of Europe: Politics, Patronage and Royalty, 1400–1800*, ed. A. G. Dickens (London, 1977); and G. Kipling, *The Triumph of Honour: Burgundian Origins of the Elizabethan Renaissance* (Leiden, 1977).

LIST OF
CONTRIBUTORS

Nigel Saul is Reader in Medieval History, Royal Holloway and Bedford New College, London. He is author of *Scenes from Provincial Life: Knightly Families in Sussex 1280–1400* (Oxford, 1986). He is currently working on a new biography of King Richard II.

Janet L. Nelson is Professor of Medieval History, King's College, London. Her *Charles the Bald* was published by Longman in 1992.

R. Allen Brown was Professor of Medieval History at King's College, London. An authority on both the Norman Conquest and the history of castles, he died in February 1989.

Deborah Kahn is Professor of the History of Art, Princeton University, New Jersey. She was a co-organizer of the Romanesque Exhibition at the Hayward Gallery in 1984.

Hugh Lawrence was Professor of Medieval History at Bedford College and later Royal Holloway and Bedford New College, London. He is the author of *St Edmund of Abingdon* (Oxford, 1960), *Medieval Monasticism* (London, 1984) and *The Friars and Medieval Society* (London, 1994).

Richard Benjamin was a research student in the University of London. He was tragically killed in a road accident in 1985.

Benjamin Arnold is Reader in Medieval History at the University of Reading. He is the author of *German Knighthood 1050–1300* (Oxford, 1985), *Princes and Territories in Medieval Germany* (Cambridge, 1991) and *Count and Bishop in Medieval Germany* (Philadelphia, 1991).

John Gillingham is Senior Lecturer in History, London School of Economics. He has published numerous books and articles on medieval history, among them *Richard the Lionheart* (2nd edn, London, 1989) and *The Angevin Empire* (London, 1984).

Robin Studd is Senior Lecturer in History and formerly Head of the Department of History at the University of Keele. He has published numerous articles on Gascon affairs in the thirteenth century.

Anthony Goodman is Professor of Medieval and Renaissance History, University of Edinburgh. His latest book, *John of Gaunt: The Exercise of Princely Power in Fourteenth-Century Europe* was published in 1992 (London).

R. R. Davies is Professor of History at the University College of Wales, Aberystwyth. He has published *Lordship and Society in the March of Wales 1282–1400* (Oxford, 1978) and *The Age of Conquest: Wales 1063–1415* (Oxford, 1991).

J. R. Maddicott is Fellow of Exeter College, Oxford. He is author of *Thomas of Lancaster 1307–22* (Oxford, 1970) and of *Simon de Montfort* (Cambridge, 1994).

Malcolm Vale is Fellow of St John's College, Oxford. A specialist in late-medieval Europe, he has written *Charles VII* (London, 1974), *War and Chivalry* (London, 1981), and *The Angevin Legacy and the Hundred Years War 1250–1340* (London, 1990).

INDEX

ILLUSTRATION ACKNOWLEDGEMENTS

The illustrations on the cover and in the plate sections have been supplied or reproduced by kind permission of the following: front cover, William the Conqueror and his barons; from a fourteenth-century manuscript (British Museum and Weidenfeld & Nicolson Archives); History Today Archives 1, 3, 22; British Library 2, 16; Michael Holford 4; A. F. Kersting 5, 6, 9, 10, 23; Conway Library and History Today Archives 7; The Pierpoint Morgan Library, New York. M.708, front cover, 8; Giraudon and History Today Archives 11; Bayer. Staatsbibliothek 12; French Government Tourist Office and History Today Archives 13; Weidenfeld & Nicolson Ltd. 14, 20; Giraudon and Weidenfeld & Nicolson Archives 15; All Souls College, Oxford and History Today Archives 17; Mansell Collection 18, 19, 21.